Beyond the Gutenberg Galaxy

MICROCOMPUTERS AND THE EMERGENCE OF POST-TYPOGRAPHIC CULTURE

Beyond the Gutenberg Galaxy

MICROCOMPUTERS AND THE EMERGENCE OF POST-TYPOGRAPHIC CULTURE

Eugene F. Provenzo, Jr.

Teachers College, Columbia University
New York and London

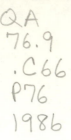
Published by Teachers College Press, 1234 Amsterdam Avenue, New York, N.Y. 10027

The cover was designed by Jan A. Kaltman. The illustration was adapted from Petrus Apianus's *Folium Populi* (1533), courtesy of the Rare Book Collection at the Library of Congress.

The capitals at the chapter openings were prepared by Catherine L. Fox from designs included in Gutenberg's Mainz Bible.

Grateful acknowledgment is extended to the MIT Press, publisher, for permission to reprint passages from Simon Nora and Alain Minc, *The Computerization of Society: A Report to the President of France*. Originally published as *L'Informatisation de la Société*, © 1978, La Documentation Française, Paris. English translation © 1980 by The Massachusetts Institute of Technology.

Library of Congress Cataloging in Publication Data

Provenzo, Eugene F.
  Beyond the Gutenberg galaxy.

  Bibliography: p.
  Includes index.
  1. Computers and civilization.   2. Microcomputers.
I. Title.
QA76.9.C66P76   1986   303.4'834   86-1938

ISBN 0-8077-2813-6

Manufactured in the United States of America

91 90 89 88 87 86   1 2 3 4 5 6

Contents

For Richard Kaeuper, *in amicitia*

Preface

THE COMPUTER, particularly as realized in the technical format of the microcomputer, has the potential to reshape not only our social and economic systems but also our traditional approaches to learning, the control of information, and the process of research. This book assumes that we are witnessing an extraordinary social and intellectual transformation in our culture that is taking place through the widespread introduction and use of computers and microcomputers. It addresses the hegemony of the computer and proposes as its basic thesis that, as the fifteenth and sixteenth centuries were defined by Gutenberg and the new technology of movable type and the book, our own era is being redefined in a similar way by the computer and the microcomputer.

The potential problems imposed by the computer and other cybernetic systems is by no means new. In the early 1950s, Norbert Weiner predicted that a new industrial revolution would come about as a result of the widespread use of automatic machines such as computers. This revolution would represent a two-edged sword, one that could be used for either the benefit or the control and manipulation of humankind. The extraordinary power of the computer to shape and define our culture requires us to make carefully considered and deliberate decisions about how and why we will make use of this new technology.

This book is written with the conviction that recent

advances in the development of computers have the potential to shape and define our educational system and culture in ways that are not sufficiently understood. Computers and microcomputers are clearly enormously valuable tools as long as we do not allow them to cripple our capacity to act as productive and creative beings. Ernest Becker, in *The Structure of Evil*, stated the problem when he argued that we must abandon the image of *l'homme machine* (human as machine). In its place we need an image of *homo poeta* (humans as meaning seekers and meaning makers). If we allow computers to limit our capacity to construct a world in which we can act productively and contribute to meaning in our lives, then we create structures that are inherently evil.[1]

In the following pages, the problems and potentials imposed by the widespread introduction and use of computers and microcomputers are analyzed in detail. In the first six chapters an attempt is made to define the key social, intellectual, and political issues that are emerging as a result of the computerization of society. These chapters are in large part a synthesis of the literature that attempts to explain the computer revolution as the key to what is described as the emergence of a "post-typographic" culture. Chapter 7 addresses the implications for education of this new model of culture and society. Chapter 8 provides a general conclusion for the book.

Throughout this book it is assumed that as a culture we are engaged in a remarkable process of change, one that we can neither easily control nor limit. While I believe that there are enormous benefits potentially provided by the new technology, the instrumental quality of the computer raises a number of serious problems. Ultimately we must adapt the computer to our needs and interests, rather than have us adapt to its organization and structure. I do not believe that this is an impossible task, only a very difficult one. It cannot be undertaken unless we begin to ask a number of critical questions about the nature of computers and how they are redefining our educational system and culture. This book is an attempt to engage us in precisely these types of questions.

Acknowledgments

I WISH to thank the many people who contributed to the writing of this book.

A sabbatical from the University of Miami during the fall of 1983 allowed me the necessary time to complete a first draft. My colleagues and students at the University of Miami —in particular, Larry LaVoie, Harland Bloland, Maria Llabre, Terry Forman, Peter Zorn, and Jay Yourist—supplied many useful ideas. Douglas Sloan, of Teachers College, Columbia University, provided insights in several informal discussions that have played an important part in shaping this book. I thank him for his interest and appreciate his different views on the role of computers in contemporary society.

Charles Campbell of the Associated Press, an old and trusted friend, patiently edited a final version of the manuscript, as did Gary McCloskey of St. Thomas University. My coresearchers, Marilyn Cohn of Washington University and Robert Kottkamp of Rutgers University, are to be thanked for their patience when I was distracted from other projects by this work.

Tom Gormley's fall 1985 fall seminar in graphic design at the University of Miami enthusiastically tackled the problem of the text and cover design for this book. Jan A. Kaltman and Catherine L. Fox deserve special thanks.

Finally, I wish to thank my wife, Asterie Baker Provenzo, for her valuable criticism and her constant support.

1 · The Emergence of Post-Typographic Culture

Any technology tends to create a new human environment.

Marshall McLuhan

N *The Gutenberg Galaxy,* Marshall McLuhan reduced the Western intellectual tradition to a single hypothesis: that the invention of movable type in the fifteenth century has been the main force in shaping Western culture.[1] This book maintains that the current proliferation and use of computers and microcomputers will be seen by future historians as a similar turning point.

Beyond the Gutenberg Galaxy is about computers and microcomputers. It is about humanity in a post-typographic culture. It assumes, as did McLuhan, that we are entering a new era—one that is being reshaped by an electronic consciousness.[2] In this context, it is the versatility and accessibility of the computer, and in particular the microcomputer, that make these machines interesting. Combined with sophisticated telecommunication systems, computers are the principal tools of post-typographic culture.

The seemingly romanticized notion that a tool such as the computer has the potential to redefine human consciousness and the character of our culture is not as unreasonable or as farfetched as it may at first seem. About one million years ago, an undistinguished "naked ape" discovered the use of tools. These were not humans but prehuman anthropoids. Tools allowed them the means by which to evolve into a higher intelligence. In this sense, "tools invented man."[3] We are at the beginning of a new phase of our history. Just as the stone axe redefined the evolution and development of prehistoric humanity, so too is the computer redefining the development and consciousness of modern women and men.

The argument that we are living at the beginning of a new computer age—as part of the millenium of the computer or the microcomputer—has been advanced many times before. Yet relatively few works have attempted to analyze in detail the social and intellectual implications of the new computer technology, and in particular the unique role of the microcomputer and its implications for education. It is the purpose of this book to do so.

Microcomputers and the Invention of Printing

There are useful parallels that can be drawn between the invention of printing and the proliferation and use of microcomputers in recent years. The changes that are beginning to emerge in our culture as a result of the large-scale introduction of microcomputers parallel many of the changes that took place in Europe as a consequence of the information revolution that followed the invention of printing.

This argument is similar to McLuhan's in *The Gutenberg Galaxy*: that modern global culture is in the process of undergoing an electronically based communications revolution whose only precedent was the typographic revolution of the fifteenth century. Unlike McLuhan, however, this work maintains that this revolution will not be based so much in media such as television, print, or the movies, but instead in the possibilities provided by the emergence and widespread availability of the new computer and microcomputer technology.

In developing this argument, the focus is on the microcomputer revolution. The ability to store, retrieve, and analyze large amounts of data, as well as to link people in complex information and communication networks, has been available through mainframe computers for nearly a quarter of a century. Yet because of their expense, the use of mainframe computers has been limited to a highly select group within the culture. Inexpensive microcomputers, with their widespread and diverse potential and their capacity to interface with mainframe computers to create telematic systems, have vastly expanded the use of computers. They are no longer the concern of a special few, but because of their accessibility and the social implications underlying their increasingly widespread use, they are the interest of an ever growing population.

It is assumed that, as a form of technology, microcomputers represent a critical force that is bringing to an end typographic culture and creating in its place a post-typographic culture and consciousness. After 500 years Western society is leaving the Gutenberg Galaxy and entering a new universe. The microcomputer is the key to this universe.

McLuhan makes only guarded references to computers in his work. He died just as microcomputers were being introduced. Even so, he seems to have clearly understood the implications of this type of technology in redefining the human experience. As he explained,

> Any technology tends to create a new human environment. Script and papyrus created the social environment we think of in connection with the empires of the ancient world. The stirrup and the wheel created unique environments of enormous scope. Technologicial environments are not merely passive containers of people but are active processes that reshape people and other technologies alike. In our time the sudden shift from the mechanical technology of the wheel to the technology of the electric circuitry represents one of the major shifts of all historical time.[4]

According to McLuhan, the invention of print created the "public," something that manuscript technology did not have the power to do.

> What we have called "nations" in recent centuries did not, and could not, precede the advent of Gutenberg technology any more than they can survive the advent of electronic circuitry with its power of totally involving all people in all other people.[5]

The extent to which the new "electronic circuitry" or consciousness will dominate our culture and create a global and interdependent village of the sort envisaged by McLuhan remains to be seen. This may in fact be more true for those engaged in intellectual activities and supported by the new microcomputer technology than for the general population. It is clear that two overlapping cultures are emerging—one characterized by typographic culture and the other, post-typographic culture. The two are neither separate nor mutually exclusive. As McLuhan pointed out in a slightly different context,

> We are today as far into the electric age as the Elizabethans had advanced into the typological and mechanical age. And we are experiencing the same confusions and indecisions which they had felt when living simultaneously in two contrasted forms of society and experience. Whereas the Elizabethans were poised between medieval corporate experience and modern individualism, we reverse their pattern by confronting an electric technology which would seem to render individualism obsolete and the corporate interdependence mandatory.[6]

The attempt here is to demonstrate that the new computer and microcomputer technology has the potential to liberate the individual as well as bind her or him to corporate interdependence. In the electronic and post-typographic culture that is superseding the typographic and mechanical era, there is the potential for new forms of human interdependence and expression to emerge. These will differ significantly from one social group to another and will bring about an important redefinition of our culture and our consciousness. At the same time, there is the potential threat to personal freedom posed by the new computer technology if it is misused or abused.

The New Generations of Computers

Computer experts describe four generations of computers that have developed, with a fifth generation to come into use in the 1990s. The first four include electronic vacuum-tube computers, transistorized computers, integrated-circuit computers, and very large-scale integrated computers (VLSI). The VLSIs are just now coming into use and will probably be superseded in the 1990s by knowledge-information-processing systems, or KIPS. These fifth-generation machines will go beyond simply processing data and be capable of symbolic manipulation and symbolic inference.[7]

The possibility of "intelligent" computers coming into widespread use in the next few years is extremely significant since they will extend computer use to an entirely new group of users. According to Edward A. Feigenbaum and Pamela McCorduck,

> Most of the world's work is nonmathematical in nature. Only a small segment of activity has as its kernel the kinds of formulas that we see in engineering and physics applications. Even in such "hard" sciences as chemistry, most thinking is done by inference, not calculation. The same is true of biology, most of medicine and all of law. Almost all the thinking of business management is done by symbolic inference, not calculation. In short, almost all the thinking that professionals do is done by reasoning, not calculating. As computing gets cheaper and the professions look to computer technologists to aid in relieving their ever-growing information processing burden, they will want to use methods that involve automated reasoning and the use of symbolic knowledge.[8]

Yet even now computers are redefining how work is done in qualitative fields such as the humanities, law, and medicine. Even when used just to process data and not to simulate "thinking," the computer has proven itself an invaluable tool.

As mentioned earlier, access to mainframe computers, because of their enormous cost, has been limited to highly select groups—the government, the scientific community, and large businesses and corporations. The introduction of microcomputers, however, has democratized computing, making computers affordable for many people for the first time. No longer is sophisticated computing an arcane and specialized art practiced by a few government officials, scientists, and business people. Computer literacy has become an important issue because such large numbers of people now have potential access to sustained computer use.

The fact that the microcomputer revolution supersedes

the computer revolution may at first seem to be just an issue of one technology succeeding another. Yet the introduction of the microcomputer represents more than just a triumph of technical ingenuity and miniaturization—it is a social and intellectual force. The invention and widespread use of the microcomputer has made possible the emergence of post-typographic culture. In years to come, microcomputers will create the basis for networks of knowledge and power that will play a crucial role in redefining the social and intellectual context in which we live.

Parallels Between the Gutenberg Revolution and the Computer Revolution

The parallels between the post-typographic revolution that is under way as a result of the introduction of the microcomputer and the typographic and print revolution that began in the Renaissance are obvious. Consider, for example, the impact of the printed book on the development of thought in fifteenth- and sixteenth-century Europe, as described by Lucien Febvre and Henri-Jean Martin. According to them, the printed book was

> one of the most potent agents at the disposal of Western civilization in bringing together the scattered ideas of representative thinkers. It rendered vital service to research by immediately transmitting results from one researcher to another; and speedily and conveniently, without laborious effort or unsupportable cost, it assembled permanently the works of the most sublime creative spirits in all fields. . . . By doing so, it gave their ideas a new lease on life and endowed them with unparalleled strength and vigour. They came to have a new kind of coherence and, by the same token, an incomparable power for both transformation and propagation. Fresh concepts crossed whole regions of the globe in the very shortest time, wherever language did not deny them access. The book created new habits of thought not only

within the small circle of the learned, but far beyond, in
the intellectual life of all who used their minds.[9]

Febvre and Martin go on to maintain that the printed book
provided a means by which to master and control the world.
In a similar vein, I maintain that the microcomputer has laid
the foundation for a revolution in thought and communication—one that will provide post-typographic society with a
radically new means by which to master information and
ideas.

There are inherent dangers in the new technology. As
McLuhan warns, "under electric technology the entire business of man becomes learning and knowing." The new
electronic technology, according to McLuhan, "requires utter
human docility and quiescence of meditation such as befits
an organism that now wears its brain outside its skull and its
nerves outside its hide."[10] Although perhaps somewhat
exaggerated, McLuhan's argument certainly deserves consideration.

Clearly, the new technology imposed by the microcomputer revolution will redefine humanity's understanding of
itself and nature. Post-typographic culture will be constrained
as well as liberated by the new technology. Knowledge,
work, and learning will be limited increasingly to the decentralized electronic network created by the microcomputer
revolution. Our culture's involvement with the electric will
be total and inclusive.[11]

Knowledge, Power, and the Book—A Historical Digression

The possession and control of information has always
been a fundamental aspect of knowledge and power. It is
true in our own era, as it was true during the late Middle
Ages. Up until the middle of the fifteenth century, books
were relatively rare objects written by hand and almost

exclusively in the possession of the Church, the universities, or the very wealthy.

Between the fall of the Roman Empire in the fourth century A.D. and the middle of the twelfth century—a period of approximately 800 years—the monasteries had almost complete control of book production and in turn the power that was endowed by the knowledge included within their pages.[12] Books were handcrafted objects, laboriously copied and reproduced in the monastic scriptoria. They were expensive and complicated affairs to produce. Besides the time that was required to copy them individually, there was the additional problem posed by the materials necessary to produce them. Paper was introduced into Europe by the Arabs via Spain and Italy at the end of the twelfth century.[13] Until this time books were written on animal hides. The raw material was expensive and the availability of hides was extremely limited. It is estimated, for example, that the hides of ten to twelve sheep were necessary to produce a manuscript book of 150 leaves measuring 24cm by 16cm.[14]

Until the beginning of the thirteenth century, the monasteries were the sole producers of books. With the rise of the universities, however, a wider readership came into existence. An active book trade began to develop in response to the demands of a growing number of scholars, teachers, and students for written material.[15]

Manuscript books remained almost exclusively under the control of either the universities or the Church. In obtaining the privilege to copy and trade books, for example, the booksellers, copyists, and stationers of late Medieval Europe were subject to the strict regulation and control of the universities. Regarded as a subgroup within the hierarchy and structure of the university system, they were awarded the protection of the universities but were not allowed to work as independent craftsmen. Essentially, they were seen as providing a service to the universities under whose administrative control they functioned.[16]

Manuscript books were usually either legal or religious

texts. Certainly the works of many classical and Arab authors were reproduced as well. Significantly, however, they were subject to censorship and control since they were reproduced by either the monastics or by the copyists under the control of the Church and the universities.

With their monopoly over the control and reproduction of written materials, the universities and the Church were able to exercise an extensive censorship "in which material suited to religion and law was given an enormous emphasis."[17] Their control was further extended as a result of their ability to define the limits and possibilities of language. Latin, the language of the Roman Empire, was also the language of the Church's empire. By controlling access to Latin, the Church and the universities in turn controlled access to knowledge.

This is not to say that Latin was the domain of the Church and the universities alone. Certainly Latin was used as the *lingua franca* of businessmen and government officials throughout the Middle Ages. However, one has only to look at the business records of the twelfth and thirteenth centuries to realize how limited the use of the language was. Highly abbreviated to save the expense of writing on vellum, frequently employing terms and phrases from the vernacular, it was not the precise, technical Latin that was the medium through which the theologians and philosophers of the late Middle Ages expressed themselves.[18]

Control of the language in which books were written, as well as the actual process of writing, had been exercised by the Church going back to the time of Charlemagne in the eighth century. In his capitularies of 787, for example, Charlemagne demanded that the clergy be required to meet higher educational standards. Uniform liturgy and ritual were established for the Church, and a revised version of the Vulgate Bible was produced using a new form of script called the Caroline minuscule. Using extensive abbreviations and suspensions, the Caroline minuscule created a type of Latin that made reading and writing an extraordinarily arcane and difficult skill.[19]

The Rise of Typographic Culture

The invention of printing redefined the power and control that the universities and the Church had throughout the late Middle Ages and the early Renaissance. With the invention of movable type and relatively inexpensive paper, books could be produced cheaply and efficiently for the first time.[20] As books became more affordable the demand for them increased. Approximately twenty million books were printed before the year 1500. This is a remarkable number when one realizes that at this time the population of Europe was certainly no greater than 100 million.[21]

The invention of printing took the book out of the nearly exclusive control of the universities and the Church and put it into the hands of the individual. The scriptoria of the monasteries and the universities were enormous and cumbersome operations—human printing presses—that existed for the sole purpose of reproducing manuscripts. The invention of printing and inexpensive paper made them obsolete. For the first time, books became relatively easy to manufacture and produce.

As long as books were expensive and rare, the demand for them was limited. As a result, until the middle of the fifteenth century there was not much pressure to produce books written and printed in languages other than Latin. Although there had been a steady increase in the written use of vernacular throughout the fourteenth and fifteenth centuries, it was the introduction of relatively inexpensive means of reproducing books that was most responsible for the increased demand for books in the vernacular. Members of the general population throughout Europe were interested in taking advantage of the new print technology and wished to do so in their own language, rather than in Latin—the language of the Church and the universities.

The parallels to the contemporary microcomputer revolution are obvious. As long as mainframe computers were limited to the use of large corporations, the government, and the universities, there was little demand from the general public for simpler computer languages and more accessible programs. Both FORTRAN and COBOL were languages written for the machines of the corporations, the government, and the universities. Knowledge of these languages was limited almost exclusively to the professional programmers who constituted the "computer priesthood."

With the recent widespread proliferation and use of microcomputers, there has emerged an increasing demand for "user-friendly" languages and programs, a development similar to the increased number of books published in the vernacular during the fifteenth and sixteenth centuries. Languages such as LOGO, specifically designed by Seymour Papert and his colleagues at the Massachusetts Institute of Technology for use with children, and the Apple Corporation's development of the LISA computer system are examples of this trend to translate computers and their use into the public vernacular.

The portability of microcomputers also has become an increasingly important issue in recent years. As microcomputers have become smaller and more compact, and as their price has decreased, the demand for portable microcomputers has increased. Portable systems the size of a small typewriter are becoming common, as are small hand-held computers. Once again there are clear parallels between the revolution that took place in the fifteenth century with the introduction of printing and the rapid dissemination and use of microcomputer technology since the late 1970s. Febvre and Martin argue that,

> thanks to printing and the multiplication of texts, the book ceased to seem a precious object to be consulted in a library: there was more and more need to be able to carry it about readily in order to refer to it or read it at any time.[22]

As its cost has decreased, the microcomputer, like the book, has come to be used more informally.

Post-Typographic Culture and the Microcomputer

The widespread use of computers, microcomputers, and the telecommunication systems that support them has redefined the possibilities of knowledge and power in our culture. For only several thousand dollars, it is suddenly possible for the private citizen, by purchasing a microcomputer, to have access to computing systems that a decade ago were almost exclusively the domain of the government, large corporations, and universities. This book was written on a microcomputer whose memory is the equivalent of IBM's famous 360 series of computers. Ironically, it is a machine that is already obsolete, having been superseded by more powerful, cheaper, and efficient microcomputers. Access by individuals to enormously powerful tools such as this have consistently had important consequences.

A case in point can be seen with the Protestant Reformation. While I would not be foolish enough to argue that the Reformation would not have taken place without the invention of the printing press and movable type, the fact may be that it would not have succeeded without them. As Febvre and Martin have commented, "One is justifiably inclined to wonder, as Henri Hauser did, what might have happened if some of the earlier heresies (the Hussite, for example) had had the power of the press at their disposal. . . ."[23]

It was through the use of the printing press that Martin Luther was able to supersede the censorship and control of the medieval church. As a result of his access to a means of producing books, he was able to present the scriptures in the vernacular to the general public, with clear consequences for the Western intellectual tradition.

The microcomputer is potentially as powerful and important a tool in the redefinition of contemporary culture as the printing press was to early modern European culture. Throughout the succeeding pages of this book there will be an attempt to explore the potential and the limitations of the microcomputer revolution, for the individual and the culture. Although the focus is on the microcomputer in particular, the analysis will also take into account the marriage between microcomputers, mainframe computers, and telecommunication systems. It is this area—the merging of microcomputer technology with mainframe computer systems and information networks to create telematic systems—that will lead to some of the most exciting and also frightening aspects of the emergence of post-typographic culture.

2 · The Information Society

The Analytical Engine weaves algebraical patterns just as the Jacquard loom weaves flowers and leaves.

Ada Augusta, Countess of Lovelace

N the previous chapter, some of the close simi-
larities between the current computer revolution
and the invention of printing were explored.
Such historical comparisons are particularly
useful, as long as they are not taken too literally.
In the following chapter, the analysis continues, in this case
examining the emergence of what the American sociologist
Daniel Bell has called "the information society." The beginning point of comparison in this chapter, however, is not the
late Middle Ages and early Renaissance, but instead the
Industrial Revolution.

The Industrial Revolution and the Computer Revolution

The Industrial Revolution began in Great Britain at the
end of the eighteenth century and rapidly spread to Europe
and North America. Within decades it transformed countries
such as Great Britain from a rural to industrial economy,
from a country of farms to a nation of cities. It brought with it
enormous social, political, and economic changes. Manufacturing, work, education, travel, and the organization and
structure of the family were among the areas that underwent
profound redefinition.

The Industrial Revolution extended the individual's
power over the environment. The invention of vehicles such
as trains and steamboats allowed people to move beyond
the limitations imposed on them by their human size and
strength, as did the use of new and complex machines in the
manufacturing of goods. In similar ways, the computer
revolution of the past few decades has extended human
power. As Christopher Evans argued,

> The Computer Revolution is the natural and proper
> successor to the Industrial Revolution, the significant
> difference being that we now move from the amplification
> and replacement of the power of muscles to the ampli-

fication and the ultimate emancipation of the power of the brain.[1]

Ironically, although it may be argued that the emergence of the computer as a powerful force within our society has only occurred since the end of the Second World War, its origin lies in the early decades of the Industrial Revolution when the English inventor and mathematician Charles Babbage first conceived of the idea of an "analytical engine."

Babbage, born in 1791, was the first individual to actually conceptualize a computer. He became interested in the idea of inventing an automatic device that could compute long lists of functions like logarithms quickly and accurately. In 1822 he presented to the Royal Astronomical Society a prototype of the machine, constructed of a series of gears and cogs and known as the Difference Engine. The Royal Society awarded Babbage a gold medal for his efforts, and he began building a full-sized version of the machine.

Babbage spent the rest of his life attempting to create his Analytical Engine. His computer was a Leviathan of cogs, belts, and wheels powered by steam engines that had to work in perfect synchronization with one another. In its final form the machine would have been the size of a football field and capable of storing one thousand fifty-digit numbers in its memory.

Babbage's machine included a logic center that manipulated data according to a specific set of rules, a memory where information was stored, and a control system for carrying out instructions. In addition, the operating procedures for the engine could be changed at will. All the elements of a modern computer were at work in Babbage's machine. Instead of being electronically based like modern computers, however, the machine was completely mechanical in nature.

Babbage was eventually assisted in his work by Ada, Countess of Lovelace, the daughter of the English poet Lord Byron. Lovelace was a gifted mathematician. When she met Babbage, she quickly realized the significance of what he was doing and began to help him in his work. Eventually, she published her reactions to his research in a work entitled "Observations on Mr. Babbage's Analytical Engine." Lovelace was remarkably canny as to the possibilities and limitations of the machine:

> The Analytical Engine has no pretensions whatever to originate anything. It can do whatever we know how to order it to perform. It can follow analysis; but it has no power of anticipating any analytical relations or truths. Its province is to assist us in making available what we are already acquainted with.[2]

Lovelace had articulated for the first time the idea of the computer as an extension of human intelligence.

To enter data into his Analytical Engine, Babbage had devised a system of punched cards similar to those used by the Frenchman Joseph Marie Jacquard to weave complex patterns into cloth. As Lovelace described the process, "The Analytical Engine weaves algebraical patterns just as the Jacquard loom weaves flowers and leaves."[3]

Unfortunately, Babbage's Analytical Engine was never completed. Many of his ideas, however, were picked up and applied by other inventors. In 1889, a young engineer named Herman Hollerith used the punch-card principle outlined by Babbage to develop a mechanical tabulating system for the U.S. Census Bureau. For the 1890 census, personal information such as the age, sex, marital status, and race of the individual was encoded and punched onto cards. These cards were then fed into Hollerith's tabulating machine where they were read by electric sensors. In 1896 Hollerith formed the Tabulating Machine Company—one of the companies that eventually formed the nucleus for the International Business Machine Corporation (IBM).[4]

The early decades of the twentieth century saw numerous advances made in the development of mechanical calculators. It was not until the 1930s, however, that Konrad Zuse, a young German engineer, constructed a simple computer that was capable of being programmed. More elaborate versions of his computer were eventually developed that employed telephone switching units and other sophisticated electrical equipment.

Zuse's research was interrupted by the Second World War. Other groups of scientists and engineers began to explore the possibilities of creating practical computers. In 1946, the first general-purpose electronic calculator was formally dedicated at the Moore School of Electrical Engineering at the University of Pennsylvania. The machine, which was designed to do ballistics calculations for the U.S. Army, was named the Electronic Numerical Integrator and Computer. Known by its initials, the ENIAC was made up of 18,000 vacuum tubes, 70,000 resistors, 10,000 capacitors, and 6,000 switches.[5] Taking up an area equivalent to a two-car garage, the machine could only work for short periods of time because its vacuum tubes kept burning out. Today, a sixteen-bit logic chip that can rest on the tip of one's finger can essentially fulfill the same and even more complex functions than the enormously cumbersome ENIAC.

Neither this book nor this chapter is intended as a history of the technical development of the computer. Instead, my purpose is to demonstrate the remarkable evolution of the computer and to reflect on its significance for our culture. In 1947, the transistor (transfer resistor) was invented by scientists at Bell Laboratories. A tiny sandwich of semiconducting materials—largely germanium crystals—was created so that a small amount of current entering one end of the transistor could control a larger amount of current in another transistor. The practical result was the creation of a simple switching device that could be used to control the flow of electrons. Much smaller than a vacuum tube, a transistor generated very little heat, was very cheap to manufacture, and rarely burned out. The first steps toward the miniaturization of the computer had taken place. By the late 1950s transistors were being etched onto tiny pieces of silicon wafer. Almost immediately, multiple transistors and the connections between them were being etched together on single slivers of silicon. The microchip had been created, and with it the possibility of putting entire sections of a computer's memory or logic system onto an incredibly tiny and efficient space.

By 1971, the microprocessor had been invented. On a single, tiny silicon chip an entire central processing unit—in essence an entire computer—was etched. The extent to which the microprocessor was an extraordinary advancement over the vacuum tubes or "valves" that were included in early computers such as the ENIAC is indicated by the following comparison made by Christopher Evans:

> To get a rough idea of what we are talking about, suppose that one expanded these tiny units up to the size of the valves in the original ENIAC and laid them side by side on a flat surface so that they would be two inches from each other, what size would this turn out to be? The answer is that it would be as big as a football field.[6]

Applications soon followed. Cheap electronic watches and extraordinarily sophisticated yet inexpensive calculators were produced. By 1975, the first microcomputer was created using microprocessors. A new phase of the computer revolution began.

With miniaturization came remarkable reductions in cost and improvements in quality. The changes that occurred since the Second World War were extraordinary. The analogy has been widely made, for example, that if the automobile industry had developed at the same rate as the computer industry over the same period of time, it would be possible to buy a Rolls Royce for $2.75 that would get three million miles to the gallon and would have enough power to drive the Queen Elizabeth II.[7]

The Redefinition of the Computer

The invention of the microprocessor, with its greater efficiency and miniature size, has made the microcomputer possible and redefined our understanding of the computer. The distinctions between mainframe and minicomputers, and between minicomputers and microcomputers, have become less clear. In many respects, the capacities of the mainframe computer of a decade ago differ little from those of the microcomputers of today.

With the invention of the integrated circuit, the microcomputer became possible. Computers no longer had to be assembled out of millions of physically different parts.

> In the new technology a complex circuit is not assembled but made as a whole, solid entity—hence the term "integrated circuit." The effect of integrated circuit technology on cost can be understood by comparing it to printing. The main expenditure of making a book occurs long before the press begins to roll. It goes into writing, editing and typesetting. Other costs occur after the printing: binding, distributing and marketing. The actual cost per copy for printing is negligible. . . . So, too, most of the cost of an integrated circuit goes into a preparatory process; the actual cost of making an individual circuit becomes negligible, provided enough are sold to spread the costs of development. The consequences of this technology for the cost of computation are dramatic. Computers that would have cost hundreds of thousands in the 1960s and tens of thousands of dollars in the early 1970s can now be made for less than a dollar.[8]

The computer could be miniaturized and mass produced at an affordable price. It was no longer an elaborate, custom-built machine. The microchip and microprocessor made it possible for computers to be "industrialized."

Information and Telecommunications in a Post-Industrial Society

In his work, *The Coming of Post-Industrial Society*, Daniel Bell has argued that since the Second World War American society has been undergoing a process of transformation from an industrially based to an information-based economy.[9] According to Bell, "The axial principle of the post-industrial society, . . . is the centrality of theoretical knowledge and its new role, when codified, as the director of social change."[10] For Bell, just as capital and labor have been the key variables in industrial society, information and knowledge have become the crucial variables in post-industrial society.[11]

Bell maintains that a new social framework based on telecommunications will probably be decisive in determining how economic and social exchanges are conducted, how knowledge is created and retrieved, and the nature of occupations in which people are engaged. The computer will play a central role in this process. In this context, according to Bell, three dimensions of post-industrial society are particularly relevant to the discussion of telecommunications and in turn the computer:

a. The change from a goods-producing to a service society
b. The centrality of the codification of theoretical knowledge for innovation in technology
c. The creation of a new "intellectual technology" as a
   key tool of systems analysis and decision theory.[12]

Implicit in Bell's prediction is a theory of communication and culture. Such an approach is by no means unique. From the nineteenth-century German philosopher and dramatist Goethe to the contemporary anthropologist Edward T. Hall, theorists have argued that communication is the basis of culture. Rather than property and production, knowledge and how it is communicated are the crucial issues in the definition of culture.

Significantly, the new communication technology—in particular the computer—represents the extension of our ability to perceive and organize knowledge. Just as the invention of writing redefined our ability to conceptualize and communicate, the computer has similarly extended what C. L. Becker has defined as our culture's "transpersonal memory."[13]

Our understanding of contemporary culture and its meaning is ultimately dependent upon our understanding of how it organizes and communicates information. In 1950, the mathematician and computer theorist Norbert Weiner wrote prophetically

> . . . that society can only be understood through a study of the messages and the communication facilities which belong to it; and in the future development of these messages and communication facilities, messages between man and machines, between machines and man, and between machine and machine, are destined to play an ever-increasing part.[14]

The complexity of contemporary culture, including the incredible expansion and growth of information, necessitates the use of tools such as computers to facilitate the organization and transmission of knowledge. Culture becomes more than just a social configuration; it is defined across the dimensions of time and space.

This idea also has been recognized by social theorists such as Harold Innis, who maintains, for example, that large-scale social and political configurations must be understood along dimensions of space and time.[15] Social and political systems, however, just as physical systems, are subject to entropy and disorganization in transit. As Norbert Weiner pointed out,

> The commands through which we exercise our control over our environment are a kind of information which we impart to it. Like any form of information, these commands are subject to disorganization in transit. They generally come through in less coherent fashion and certainly not more coherently than they were sent. In control and communication we are always fighting nature's tendency to degrade the organized and to destroy the meaningful; the tendency as Gibbs has shown us, for entropy to increase.[16]

Translated into practical terms, Weiner is arguing that what starts out as information at the upper level of a hierarchy is transformed and distorted as part of the attempt to communicate it to the lower levels of the system. In a similar way, as messages are successively transferred within any social or cultural system, their meaning becomes less clear and precise.

The computer—and more specifically the microcomputer —can do much to alleviate the distortion of knowledge and information in our culture by providing individuals with greater access to sources of data and the means by which to analyze them. An example can be seen with the reporting of stock market information. Rather than being dependent upon generalized summaries provided by a stockbroker via newspaper, radio, or television, a private individual can have direct access to online financial information. Using a system such as CompuServe, a private individual can compile detailed, undistorted information on a particular stock and make personal financial decisions without professional assistance.

The development and increasingly widespread use of telematic systems brings with it a number of important questions: Who controls sources of information? How are they defined? Who has access to them? These are extraordinarily important issues that will play a crucial role in defining the nature and purpose of our culture.

The Emergence of a New Literacy

At the conclusion of *The Gutenberg Galaxy*, Marshall McLuhan asked what new mechanisms and configurations of literacy would emerge as our traditional culture merged with "the new electric age."[17] Clearly, the new electronic technology has begun to redefine our traditional formulations of knowledge and learning. With the emergence of post-typographic culture—what Bell chooses to describe as the "information society"[18]—we bring to its final conclusion a process that began with the Industrial Revolution. We have gone beyond the mechanical technologies of the eighteenth and nineteenth centuries, which extended the physical power of human beings. In place of a revolution based upon external manifestations of power, we are confronted with an internal revolution involving the extensions of our culture, one prophetically anticipated by McLuhan:

> Today, after more than a century of electric technology, we have extended our central nervous system itself in a global embrace, abolishing both space and time as far as our planet is concerned. Rapidly, we approach the final phase of the extensions of man—the technological simulation of consciousness. . . .[19]

Like Calaban in *The Tempest*, we are faced with a "brave new world." It is a world in which power and knowledge are still being defined.

Clearly the computer and the microcomputer offer the potential for improving the condition of humanity. At the same time, their inappropriate use poses a potential threat to the most fundamental social and moral foundations of our culture. Critical and far-reaching questions must be asked about how and why we are using the new technology. Like the educational historian and social theorist Douglas Sloan, I feel strongly that

> American educators have made no concerted effort to ask at what level, for what purposes, and in what ways the computer is educationally appropriate or inappropriate, in what ways and to whom we can count on its being beneficial or harmful.[20]

Important questions need to be raised concerning the appropriate use of computers within our culture and society. Will people be different as a result of having ready access to computers? What are the potential dangers posed by the new technology in terms of the manipulation and control of information? Will the widespread use of computers and online information systems lead to the reorganization of traditional knowledge systems? Will the use of the new technology alter the way in which we understand the world around us, perhaps eventually leading to a redefinition of our consciousness? What do we gain and what do we sacrifice by emphasizing the use of computers as an important part of the curriculum of our schools? Will technical reason predominate to the detriment of other human capacities? We must not forget that

> cognition involves a rationality much deeper and more capacious than technical reason . . . that even the development of strong logic and technical reason itself may not best be served by the hot-house forcing of analytical and abstract thinking at an even earlier age.[21]

Nearly four decades ago, the mathematician Norbert Weiner called for "the human use of human beings." The key question that must be addressed concerning the use of computers and microcomputers in years to come is, What is their appropriate use, and how can they best help us realize our humanity? The challenge of living in a post-typographic culture is how best to take advantage of the opportunities provided by the new technology, without diminishing ourselves as humans. In doing so, we must come to see the computer not only as a technological innovation but also as a social and moral force within our culture. Ultimately, we must ask ourselves whether or not the technical reason of the computer can be separated from our moral and aesthetic sensibilities.

3 · Microcomputers and Telematic Consciousness

The computer is not the only technological innovation of recent years, but it does constitute the common factor that speeds the development of all others.

Simon Nora and Alain Minc

HE emergence of post-typographic culture is a social and cultural phenomenon that is a direct consequence of the widespread proliferation and use of computers and microcomputers. Although in years to come other technological innovations such as recombinant DNA research and atomic fusion have the potential to change and alter the direction of our culture radically, neither seems to possess the same potential as the computer to redefine "the entire nervous system of social organization."[1]

Yet despite the potential of the computer, and in particular the microcomputer, to redefine our consciousness, it is the linking of computers and microcomputers through information networks that will be most responsible for redefining our culture. Just as the harnessing of steam power was the necessary condition for the creation of an industrial society, so too will the harnessing of computer power be the necessary condition for the creation of an information-based or post-typographic culture.

Significantly, this will be a synergistic process in which widely different technological innovations will be merged together to create a single and dynamic social force. In particular, computers and microcomputers will be merged with telecommunication systems—a process the French have described as "telematique" or, in English, "telematics."

Telematics and Post-Typographic Culture

Telematics represents the merging of computers and microcomputers with major data banks and transmission systems. Although such systems have been available to government and scientific research groups on mainframe computers for at least two decades, they have only just begun to be made available to most academic researchers and the public in general. Through electronic networks, data processing is becoming available to the general population for the first time.

Using a microcomputer with a modem, it has become possible for private individuals to reach major national data bases through systems such as CompuServe, Viewtron, and DIALOG. In the case of DIALOG, for example, which can be accessed in a matter of minutes on the same microcomputer system used to write this book, it is possible to explore 150 different data bases containing a total of 55 million records. Data bases for the system include an incredibly diverse set of formats, from technical reports and conference papers to patent designs and journal articles, just to name a few. Data bases are available for education, science, business, finance, current affairs, social science, law, medicine, the arts, and the humanities.[2]

The cost for using the system, although not cheap, is well within the range of most individuals. A five-minute computer bibliographical search of a data base with 20,000 documents costs approximately $5 or $6.[3] Bibliographical research that would have taken literally hundreds of hours in the past can be done in a few hours. In most instances, more effort is devoted to organizing the search (selecting categories, key names, and so on) than actually using the computer.

Sources such as DIALOG are not only changing the means by which research is conducted, but they are rapidly redefining the research process. Those academics, for example, who do not quickly adapt themselves to using online bibliographical systems are not going to be able to be competitive with their colleagues who are using these systems. Not only will they be working much less efficiently, but the material they collect will be much less current and complete.

The widespread use of data processing by professional researchers has been a relatively limited phenomenon, in part because it was so expensive. As Simon Nora and Alain Minc have explained,

> Until fairly recently, data processing was expensive, unreliable and esoteric, restricted to a limited number of businesses and operations. Data processing was elitist, a prerogative of the great and powerful. Henceforth, mass

computerization will take hold, becoming as indispensable
to society as electricity.[4]

It is significant that, as professionals turn to cheap sources of
information via the computer as a means of coping with the
demands of their work, the cost of using various information
systems will become even cheaper and more widespread.
Computers and online information systems have the potential to become as common as the telephone. One can
envisage groups ranging from professional researchers to
hobbyists, spread across the country and even the world,
compiling enormous, shared data bases involving mutual
areas of interest. One need only explore the electronic bulletin
boards that have been set up in recent years by various
microcomputer organizations and groups across the country
to realize what the possibilities might be for other groups five
or ten years from now.

It is important to note that such systems will be inter-
active, allowing individuals from different regions and with
different experiences and backgrounds to communicate and
pool resources in mutually agreed upon areas. Activities
might be as simple as cataloguing baseball cards or some type
of antique or collectible, or they might involve pooling joint
information for political purposes, or developing a definitive
scholarly bibliography on DNA research or the poetry of
John Milton.

Telematics and Expert Knowledge

Telematics, or networking, could restructure our work
and culture. It gives people a way to maintain and promote
their autonomy. Peripheral groups, or isolated units within
the culture, can suddenly take advantage of data bases that
previously had only been available to major organizations.[5]
An example can be seen with scholars isolated from major
university libraries. In scholarly areas such as history, the
creation of knowledge is critically dependent upon access to

primary and secondary sources. As a result, the ability of scholars to undertake original research is directly related to the quality of the libraries within the regions in which they live and work. While relatively inexpensive air travel, inter-library loan, and microfilm have made this less of an issue in recent years, lack of easily accessible sources has undoubtedly limited the productivity of many scholars. Online information and video-disc data-storage systems are making major collections such as the Library of Congress available on a national basis. While still in their early phases of development, such systems should become standard by the early or mid 1990s.

Expert knowledge becomes redefined and more accessible to the general population. A case in point can be seen with the legal profession. Like most professions, the law has maintained its professional authority largely as a result of expert knowledge. Researching legal precedents and drawing up documents such as business contracts and wills have been among the principal activities of the legal profession. New computer programs, many of which are designed for use with microcomputers, in addition to computer reference services, now enable lay persons to do much of the work that was traditionally conducted by lawyers. Menu-driven programs are now being commercially distributed that allow the user to create a will, as well as certain types of contracts. Online reference services such as LEXIS and WestLaw, although more difficult to access, now make highly complex legal research possible for the private individual. In the area of patent searches, for example, it is no longer necessary to employ a lawyer or patent researcher in Washington or at a secondary depository to trace a patent. Instead, an online data base—employing either a standard terminal with a modem or microcomputer with a modem—can be used to consult sources such as the U.S. Patent Abstracts.[6]

Typesetting is a different example. Historically, it has been a highly specialized craft that has demanded long years of training and apprenticeship. As a result the cost of setting type for printing, a largely labor-intensive activity, has been relatively expensive. In recent years the costs of typesetting have come down considerably as a result of the introduction of computers and then minicomputers. Metal cast typesetting, the tradition since Gutenberg, has become an oddity. In its place, sophisticated, computer-driven photolithography systems have taken over the industry.

While computer typesetting systems were initially extremely expensive and dependent upon mainframe computers, they have become increasingly compact and efficient in recent years. Typesetting systems are suddenly being interfaced with microcomputers, so authors can prepare their own texts for printing, largely bypassing the typesetter. A data file can be easily transferred by disk or modem to the memory of the typesetting computer. Minor corrections and alterations can be made, and the text can be run off as galleys from a printer.

Telecommunication systems, moreover, make it possible to transmit the text from a microcomputer to a typesetter anywhere in the country. For example, a manuscript could be written on a microcomputer in Florida, transmitted to New York to be edited by a publisher, and then transmitted back to Florida to have typesetting commands inserted (which also could have been done as part of the editorial process in New York). The manuscript could next be transmitted to a typesetter in another state, such as Vermont or New Hampshire where labor costs might be cheaper, to have the text run off in the typeface selected as galleys on a photoprinter.

Such methods, besides being economically worthwhile, introduce a whole new element into the production of the book. With books involving elaborate visual design, sophisticated typography, and related types of input, the process remains much more in the hands of the author. In this sense, telematics has reintroduced a series of procedures for the manufacturing of books that is reminiscent of the early history of printing, when author/printers such as William Caxton crafted books by handling the entire process from writing through typesetting, even to the final printing.

Other examples in many different fields could be used to

elaborate further. What is crucial, however, is the realization that the telematic process—in which individuals are given access to "intelligent" terminals in the form of microcomputers that are linked to sophisticated communication systems—suddenly makes it possible for them to become much more autonomous from the traditional hierarchical structure. As a result, creativity can be much more individualized and independent.

The Decentralization of Data Processing

The introduction of the microcomputer and the development of telematic systems will lead increasingly to the redefinition of traditional structures of knowledge and power. Existing information hierarchies will be redefined. These redefinitions will carry with them profound social implications. As Nora and Minc explain,

> Information technology has today become an almost completely flexible tool. Its organization can spread without encountering a major obstacle through all the configurations of power. It will disrupt the rules and conditions governing competition among numerous economic agents; it will confirm or annul the status of positions between the center and periphery in most organizations. But this diffused penetration will involve deep changes in essential functions (medicine, education, law, Social Security, working conditions) and by increasing transparency will raise the question of security and privileges that issue from the shadowy zone of society.[7]

The microcomputer and telematic revolution—the realization of a post-typographic culture—has the potential to redefine radically the traditional lines of organization and authority. The microcomputer and telematics also have the potential to redefine hierarchical structures at all levels of the society. According to Nora and Minc,

Traditional data processing was hierarchical, isolated and centralized. The technical constraints were prejudicial in terms of the mode of organization which it imposed, because the presence of computers relieved the natural weightiness of the enterprises and administrations. Indeed, its procedures reinforced the center to the detriment of the periphery and the higher executive level to the detriment of the smallest units of management.[8]

In a remarkable turnabout, the microcomputer, linked creatively with telecommunication systems, has the potential to precisely reverse this process. As a result of the new technology, data processing can become decentralized and autonomous.[9] A private individual using a microcomputer with a modem can be linked to a virtually unlimited number of data bases, analyze information without the constraints imposed by a larger organizational or bureaucratic structure, and use the results in whatever way she or he likes.

George Orwell and Big Brother

The argument up until this point has been highly optimistic, assuming that entrenched bureaucracies will not interfere with the flow of information and communication now possible in our culture. It is interesting to speculate, for example, what the impact of microcomputers and telematics might be on a totalitarian society such as the Soviet Union. One would assume that access to data banks, the creation of information networks, and the free flow of ideas promoted by the new computer technology would pose an inherent threat to the existing economic, social, and class structure within the Soviet Union. An alternative scenario is possible, however, one that has important implications for our own culture. The careful regulation and control of data bases, accessed by "dumb" rather than "intelligent" terminals, could provide an enormously effective means of regulating and controlling information and ideas within the culture.

An example of how this could take place was anticipated by George Orwell in his novel, *1984*. Orwell did not include computers in his fictional description of a totalitarian Western Europe; however, Orwell's principal character, Winston Smith, works in the Ministry of Truth where he rewrites history in order to suit current propaganda needs. As long as information has been received and preserved largely through printed sources, such censorship has never been practical, because too many copies of documents contradicting the revised "history" survive. But in a centrally controlled data base it becomes extremely easy to manipulate such data. A name removed, a date changed, or some other piece of information altered, and all subsequent reports drawn from the data base incorporate the revisions.

Using such techniques, the controversial publications of a particular author could be removed from access to the public. History could be rewritten—names altered, dates changed, events forgotten—and no one except those responsible for changing the data base would necessarily know the difference. Once a generation had come to pass, the changes would be known to no one.

David Burnham, in his book, *The Rise of the Computer State*, describes in detail the possibilities of such abuse, not in the Soviet Union, but in the United States.[10] According to Burnham, in our uncritical search for greater efficiency and productivity, we have accepted the computer without carefully considering the implications and possible abuses that the records it creates have for personal privacy and freedom. He cites the mathematician and inventor of cybernetics, Norbert Weiner, as saying that "progress imposes not only new possibilities for the future, but new restrictions. The simple faith in progress is not a conviction belonging to strength but belonging to acquiescence and hence to weakness."[11] Weiner proceeds to argue that machines such as computers "do and can transcend some of the limitations of their designers and that in doing so they may be both effective and dangerous."[12]

Burnham argues, quite correctly, that the computer and telecommunications have encouraged the transfer of vast amounts of personal and private information. Bank records, credit card bills, and income tax returns, to mention just a few sources of computerized data, provide precise information on the travels, purchases, and activities of individuals. When made available to government or other sources without the knowledge and consent of the individual, they pose a particular threat to personal privacy and freedom.

Burnham rejects the notion

> that the rapid growth in the use of personal computers by millions of American citizens will cancel out the increases in power flowing to large organizations. This defense has surface plausibility. But when the vast capital, expertise and manpower available to the large government and business organizations are compared to the capital, expertise and available working time of even the most favored individual, the personal computer does not appear to be a great equalizer.[13]

The impact of the microcomputer revolution and telematics on contemporary social organization and political control is an issue whose outcomes are yet to be decided. There is no doubt that uncontrolled government access to data bases and the manipulation and abuse of these systems can lead to tremendous infringement of personal rights and freedoms. Yet at the same time, as Nora and Minc point out, such systems can also provide for the broader and more democratic distribution of information.[14]

Telematics and the Redefinition of Culture

Changes in the structure and organization of knowledge inevitably lead to the redefinition of culture. The rise of the mechanically printed book, beginning in the fifteenth century, led to the increasing empowerment of the middle class, just as the appearance of economics, sociology, and psychology in our own era contributed to the growth of a new technocratic class.[15] How microcomputers and the telematic revolution will define the culture will be in many respects determined by how we allow them to be used. At the present time, critically important decisions are being made concerning the adoption and use of computers that will influence not only ourselves but future generations as well.

In the past, we have adopted technologies with little or no consideration of the consequences of their use. Douglas Sloan, in questioning the extent to which we should be cautious in adopting the new computer and microcomputer technology, points to the automobile as an example of a supposedly beneficial and benign technology that has brought with it huge personal, social, and environmental costs.[16] The widespread adoption and use of the automobile has shaped the design of our cities and suburbs, led to the pollution of much of our environment, and made us dependent upon foreign nations for oil.

Precedents that are currently being set in terms of computer use are likely to continue to influence us in years to come. Many issues that are seemingly trivial at present may in fact take on greater significance with the passage of time. An example can be seen with something as simple as the automatic, computerized dialing and advertising systems that have come into widespread use in recent years. With one of these systems, telephone numbers can be dialed automatically for every number in an exchange, whether they are listed or unlisted. When the phone is answered, a recorded message is played. Until the message is finished and the computer disconnects the line, there is no way of breaking the connection by the call's receiver. No other call, whether for business, an emergency, or personal use, can be made.

Clearly the use of such advertising systems represents a serious infringement upon the rights of the individual. Taken to an extreme, one can envisage a constant flood of automatic phone calls that are impossible to shut off. Fortunately, many states have begun to make it illegal to use such systems. In doing so, a deliberate decision has been made to restrict the use of an available technology in order to protect the rights of private citizens.

Ultimately we are faced with the challenge of developing a social and technical system that will allow information collection and dissemination and social organization to progress alongside one another. Post-typographic culture remains in the process of formulation. Through the micro-computer, the computer, and telematic systems, we have the potential to promote personal freedom or restrict it. We need to proceed cautiously in the adoption and use of computers and microcomputers within our culture. It is our obligation to consider questions about how much information we need to have access to and how we use that information.

4 · Microcomputers and the Neo-Luddites

Are we not ourselves creating our successors, . . . daily giving them greater skill and supplying more and more of that self-regulating, self-acting power which will be better than any intellect?

Samuel Butler

N Arthur C. Clarke's *2001: A Space Odyssey*, the spaceship's sentient computer, HAL, murders the spaceship's crew.[1] As in Mary Shelley's gothic horror story, *Frankenstein, or the Modern Prometheus*, an intelligent, almost-human scientific creation goes out of control and destroys the very individuals whom it is intended to protect and serve.[2] Like Shelley's *Frankenstein*, Clarke's *2001* raises not only the question of what is "consciousness," but also the issue of humankind's profound distrust of its own creations, particularly those that closely imitate human life.

The distrust of computers is a reflection of a series of tensions that have always existed between humans and machines. During the early part of the Industrial Revolution in England, workers protesting the introduction of labor-saving machines, such as Arkwright's water frames and carding engines, destroyed the machines in order to protect their jobs. Even at that time, hostility to the introduction of mechanized and partially automated industrial processes was not a new phenomenon in England. Legislation from the late medieval period throughout the modern era suggests that opposition on the part of workers to the introduction of new technologies was a frequent and widespread problem.[3] Machine breaking or the threat of it during the late eighteenth and early nineteenth centuries probably provided the basis of power for many of the early English trade unions.[4]

The workers who destroyed machines during the early phases of the Industrial Revolution in England have come to be known as Luddites. The origin of their name seems to come from a series of letters threatening English factory owners that were circulated in 1811 under the name "Ned Ludd."[5] In fact, the Luddites represented many different groups and interests. If they were at all unified by a single characteristic, it was their opposition to workers being displaced in the industrial system by improved machines and technologies.[6]

In this chapter, the term *neo-Luddite* is used to describe the significant opposition that has developed among many people to the proliferation and increasingly widespread use of mainframe computers and microcomputers in our culture. Clearly the parallel between the Luddites and what we are calling the neo-Luddites is highly generalized. Yet, in many respects, each group represents a similar response to displacement and other problems of social and economic change caused by the introduction of new technologies.

Computers and the Transformation of Culture

Contemporary opposition and distrust of the new computer technology is not without justification. Clearly the potential exists for the misuse of information organized and collected by computers, their displacement and redefinition of the workforce, and their reinforcement of already powerful bureaucratic structures within the government and the business sector. Opponents argue that the increased computerization of society represents, according to Nora and Minc,

> a victory for the impersonal, repetitive nature of tasks and the elimination of jobs. It would solidify the unwieldiness and hierarchical nature of organizations, reinforcing the omniscience of those "in the know" while automatizing the others. All that would remain would be the computers and the computerized, the users and the used. The machine would no longer be a computer (*ordinateur*), a tool for calculating, remembering and communicating, but a mysterious and anonymous order-giver (*ordonnateur*).[7]

Society would, according to the neo-Luddite view, become less and less comprehensible to its members, more subject to manipulation by an elite, and ultimately less free.[8]

In contrast, those optimistic about the new computer technology believe that the computer will revolutionize the organization and distribution of information. Accepting the neo-Baconian point of view that knowledge leads inevitably to progress and power, they are little bothered by the possible misuse and abuse of the new technology. According to them, the computer means information and an information society. Through the further definition and elaboration of culture, democracy and personal freedom will be served.[9]

Clearly, the uncritical acceptance of the computer is as dangerous as its rejection. The challenge of post-typographic culture is to build a "system of connections that will allow information and social organization to progress together."[10] Computerization can either help or impede this process. The question of how we adopt and use the computer is in fact part of a larger question that asks what the future of society itself will be. Will a culture based on high productivity be stable or not? Will we see a gradual erosion of tradition and the realignment of power?[11]

The new information society that is emerging implies the negation of traditional political philosophies. Marxist theory, for example, is based upon the premise that the opposition between the working class and the bourgeoisie is economically based. Yet it is clear, as pointed out by Nora and Minc, that, as modes of production are replaced through automation (that is, computerization), traditional sources of class conflict should be eliminated. Instead of economic capital, power could be defined by a new capital—information.[12]

Liberal culture in contrast, according to Nora and Minc, assumes that a postindustrial society will evolve toward an ideal of greater social and political equity. Essentially, it is assumed that the wealth provided by a computerized society's greater productivity will create a classless and content homogeneous society characterized by leisure and personal freedom.[13]

Neither the liberal nor Marxist scenario seems realistic. Post-typographic culture will see the individual facing a series of social and political questions that go beyond traditional political ideologies and social structures. We are in the process of undergoing a redefinition of our models of culture and society. What might eventually emerge in the Soviet Union or China, based on the assumptions of their political systems, are cultures not unlike the totalitarian systems described by Aldous Huxley in *Brave New World* or George Orwell in *1984*.[14]

Clearly, the automation of society has the potential to create the leisured and contented hierarchies of Alphas and Betas that made possible Huxley's hedonistic but carefully circumscribed *Brave New World*. In a like fashion, the existence of the computer could make a reality of Orwell's vision of the future in which Big Brother constantly watches over everyone, in which history is rewritten to serve the needs of the moment, and in which personal freedom and individuality are denied for the betterment of collective culture.

Samuel Butler, "Erewhon," and the Book of the Machines

Ironically, neither Huxley nor Orwell predicted the coming of computers. In fact, of all the technologies anticipated by philosophers and writers during the past two centuries, perhaps none has been less predicted than the computer. An exception to this is Samuel Butler's utopian novel, *Erewhon*, in which the significance of the impact of "intelligent" machines on his imaginary culture is examined in great detail.[15]

The first part of *Erewhon* to be written was published as a newspaper article in *The Press* (Christchurch, New Zealand) in June of 1863. Entitled "Darwin Among the Machines," the article later became the basis for "The Book of the Machines," included by Butler in the second half of *Erewhon*.[16] Although Butler in no way specifically anticipates computers as such, he does anticipate the extraordinarily rapid evolution of intelligent machines. In the land of Erewhon ("nowhere" roughly spelled backwards), all machines have been banished. Having begun to develop an advanced technological culture, the Erewhonians realized that machines were evolving more quickly than humanity. In doing so, the Erewhonians saw that the evolution of machines posed a threat to their own personal and human development.

According to the unnamed author of "The Book of the

Machines," the most important and sacred of all Erewhon's literature,

> There is no security . . . against the ultimate development of mechanical consciousness, in the fact of machines possessing little consciousness now. A mollusc has not much consciousness. Reflect upon the extraordinary advance which machines have made during the last few hundred years, and note how slowly the animal and vegetable kingdoms are advancing. The more highly organised machines are creatures not so much of yesterday, as of the last five minutes, so to speak, in comparison with past time.[17]

Without in any way specifically anticipating the computer, Butler clearly understood the potentially rapid evolution of "machine intelligence." As his author of "The Book of the Machines" makes clear, the concern is, not with the intelligence of any existing machine, but instead with the intelligence toward which the machine is rapidly evolving:

> Do not let me be misunderstood as living in fear of any actually existing machine; there is probably no known machine which is more than a prototype of future mechanical life. The present machines are to the future as the Saurians [dinosaurs] to man. The largest of them will probably greatly diminish in size. Some of the lowest vertebrata attained a much greater bulk than has descended to their more highly organized living representatives, and in like manner a diminution in the size of machines has often led to their development and progress.[18]

The computer and more specifically the microcomputer are the fulfillments of Butler's prophecy.

The consistency and dependability of machines and their intelligence are among their greatest threats. As the author of "The Book of the Machine" explains,

> Whenever precision is required man flies to the machine at once, as far preferable to himself. Our sum-engines

never drop a figure, nor our looms a stitch; the machine is brisk and active, when the man is weary; it is clearheaded and collected, when the man is stupid and dull; it needs no slumber, when man must sleep or drop; ever at its post, ever ready for work, its alacrity never flags, its patience never gives in; its might is stronger than combined hundreds, and swifter than the flight of birds.[19]

In time, the machine no longer simply serves the individual but shapes and directs the purpose of humanity. The consciousness of the machine supersedes the individual's consciousness. Eventually people come to serve the machine instead of themselves. Butler asks:

How many men at this hour are living in a state of bondage to the machines? How many spend their whole lives from cradle to the grave, in tending them by night and by day? Is it not clear that the machines are gaining ground upon us, when we reflect upon the increasing number of those who are bound down to them as slaves, and of those who devote their whole souls to the advancement of the mechanical kingdom?[20]

Artificial Intelligence and the Definition of the Individual

The fear, outlined by Butler in *Erewhon*, of machines superseding people is not without reason. It is clear that the field of artificial intelligence is advancing so rapidly that the sharply demarcated lines that have separated humans from machines are becoming less clear.

In our own era, some of the most potentially exciting and provocative intellectual inquiries being undertaken involve the meaning of "machine consciousness" and "human consciousness"—a question that in fact has its origins in the mind/body problem posed by the French philosopher Rene Descartes over 400 years ago and characterized by his famous proposition, "Cognito ergo sum" ("I think, therefore I exist").[21]

It is clear that the traditional wisdom that computers are simply gigantic but ultimately stupid machines is changing. As Butler predicted, the evolution of the computer (that is, the machine) is advancing more rapidly than human evolution. Yet one can make the counterargument that machines such as computers are partners in human evolution. As discussed earlier, humankind has evolved as a species through the use of tools. *Homo faber*, "man the maker," is a nomenclature that describes humanity's evolution from a primitive to a modern being. Assuming that the computer is simply another of humankind's tools—an extension of human intelligence—then the real threat posed by the computer is not what it can do but what it is allowed to do.

In his collection of science fiction stories, *I Robot*, Isaac Asimov addresses the question of creating super intelligent machines that will serve people but not supersede them.[22] He does this by framing his three now-famous "Laws of Robotics." The first and most important of these laws is that a robot must not harm, or through inactivity allow to come to harm, a human being. The second law states that a robot must obey all commands given to it by a human being except when these conflict with the first law. The third law finally states that a robot must preserve itself at all times unless by doing so it contradicts the first two laws.[23] Through the use of these three laws Asimov is able to create a world in which humans and computers (that is, robots) can exist and benefit one another.

As computers continue to evolve, one wonders if it will be feasible to build such safeguards into our society. Clearly this issue will be determined to some extent by how computers are used. In the recent movie and novel, *WarGames*, for example, a teenage microcomputer enthusiast accidentally triggers an air-defense computer into going to war. Although it is soon realized that a terrible mistake has been made, the computer is programmed to override any outside interference. In essence, the computer was unable to distinguish between a war game and real war and came perilously close to starting World War III.[24] *WarGames* has been criticized for presenting an impossible scenario of what could happen if a computer system got out of control. One wonders, however, as computers become more "intelligent" and operate more and more at the levels of decision making and analysis, if the possibilities of such an event taking place will become more feasible.

An even more chilling scenario, also the subject of a motion picture, is presented in the Walt Disney feature film, *Tron*. Here a "master control program" sets out on a program of conquest in which it invades the memories of other computers by means of various telecommunication systems and absorbs them into its own memory. While science fiction for the present, one wonders whether or not the possibility of a military computer system being taken over by an invading machine consciousness may not be very plausible in the not-too-distant future. If such a situation were to come to pass, it would represent Butler's worst fears of humanity being dominated by the machine.

Distinctions Between Humans and Machines

If one assumes that the mind is the essence of humanity and computers in the very near future are going to be able to think or simulate thought, then what is it that will define the difference between humans and machines? Many traditional religions would define the difference as the human possession of a soul. The issue is addressed in *Frankenstein*, when the monster poses the question: "I live, I breathe, I walk, I see—but what am I, Man or Monster?" Is the question really that different with the superintelligent computers that are likely to be developed in the coming decades?

In Arthur C. Clarke's *2001: A Space Odyssey*, the HAL 9000 computer runs wild, killing the members of the spaceship's crew. The last survivor, Dave, manages to get access to the computer's main memory. First he destroys the "cognitive-feedback" and then the "ego-reinforcement" systems of the computer's memory. As HAL proceeds to lose more and more of his memory and consciousness, he asks Dave to stop shutting him down, explaining that he is afraid of what is happening to him.

> And at these words he had indeed stopped—though only for a moment. There was a poignancy in that simple phrase that struck to his heart. Could it be only an illusion, or some trick of subtle programming—or was there a sense in which HAL really was afraid? But this was no time to indulge in philosophical hair-splitting.[25]

For just a moment Dave asks himself what "feel" really means to a computer. A few moments later the computer's program was erased.

In *Erewhon*, Samuel Butler wonders whether it can be true that, "because the life of machines is a very different one to our own, there is therefore no higher possible development of life than ours; or that because mechanical life is a very different thing from ours, therefore that it is not life at all."[26] The computer is the first machine that may supersede our ability fully to encompass or understand it and its possible consciousness. It is little wonder that, besides being concerned about the computer's ability to change the fundamental social and economic conditions of our society, we also distrust its imitation of what we believe perhaps most clearly and distinctly defines our humanity.

The computer is redefining our understanding of ourselves and our consciousness. If we distrust the computer, it is because we distrust ourselves and what we do with our machines. The computer, how it is used, and the conditions placed upon the rapid evolution of its "intelligence" pose what are among the most interesting issues facing our culture in the final decades of the twentieth century. How we cope with the computer and its various ramifications will in the end come to define humanity in a post-typographic culture.

5 · The Electronic Scriptorium

*In the long run it is ideas and not men
who rule the world.*

John Maynard Keynes

N the Middle Ages, sophisticated networks of knowledge and information existed as a result of itinerant and wandering scholars traveling on a regular basis from one university and monastic center to another, collecting information and exchanging ideas. The linking of intellectual centers by wandering scholars undoubtedly contributed to the intellectual flowering of the twelfth century. The works of Aristotle and other ancients, whose ideas had been lost for nearly a millennium, were rediscovered in Arab libraries, carried back to Europe, and translated. A medieval renaissance—a flowering of philosophy, mathematics, and science —resulted. Adelard of Bath, Peter Abelard, Roger Bacon, and St. Thomas Aquinas are among the extraordinary figures who emerged during this period.

What is particularly important in light of my discussion up until this time is that this medieval renaissance was made possible by the exchange of ideas between different intellectual centers. In essence, it was communication that set in motion what are widely considered among the greatest intellectual accomplishments of the Middle Ages.

In our own era, as a result of the development of the microcomputer and telematic systems, we are witnessing what future intellectual and social historians will almost certainly regard as an equally important revolution in communication and scholarship. As we go beyond the Gutenberg Galaxy and enter a post-typographic culture, we will see the traditional methods and results of scholarship redefined. Through the establishment of information networks and knowledge pathways made possible by the microcomputer and telematic systems, we will have the potential to extend and refine intellectual discourse in a manner that has never been possible before.

Overcoming Barriers of Time and Space

I have chosen the phrase *electronic scriptorium* to describe the new knowledge pathways that have come into being as a result of the microcomputer and the telematic revolution. In selecting this term, I am conscious of the parallels between the pursuit of knowledge by the monastic and university scholars of the high Middle Ages and early Renaissance and the scholars and researchers of the late twentieth and early twenty-first centuries.

Like the wandering scholars of the eleventh and twelfth centuries, the freedom provided to contemporary scholars as a result of the creation of new information pathways is enormous. Existing computer networking systems have suddenly made it possible to link scholars together from widely different geographical regions in what is essentially an invisible college or university.

Using microcomputer or mainframe terminals linked by modems via the telephone system it is now possible not only to maintain continuous communication and information exchanges but also to draw on very large and sophisticated data bases. Geographically separated groups are able to communicate with each other conveniently and at relatively small cost. A permanent record is maintained of all proceedings. Systems are asynchronous, meaning that problems created by barriers of time and space are eliminated and that people can participate in a system at a time and place that are most convenient for them.[1] Scholars and researchers linked by computers provide the potential for a major advance in the development and diffusion of knowledge in almost all fields.

Such a system might work as follows. A group of scholars interested in a common topic and located at various universities or research centers across the country (or the world) would decide to pursue an area of discussion or research with one another. A networking and conference program linking the scholars would be set up and a dialogue begun.[2] In such a system, messages could be sent to an individual, a selected group, or to everyone in the system. Anonymity, if desired, would be possible, making a freer expression of opinions possible. Discussions of topics could be held in "real time" (synchronous time), with scholars transmitting comments or opinions back and forth over the transmission lines;

or talks could be held over a period of several days, weeks, or even years (asynchronous time). Special documents or notes could be stored in the system for members to refer to, and an "electronic bulletin board" could provide the space for special reports, notes, or messages. A text editor would make possible the joint writing and drafting of documents.[3]

This type of system would introduce a new dynamic into traditional exchanges of information. Scholars would not have much of an incentive to input information unless they had something important to say. Anyone who has worked on a committee of scholars knows that to a certain extent many of the presentations and exchanges that scholars make are done in order to demonstrate one's knowledge of the literature or one's cleverness as a researcher. Such demonstrations become largely meaningless in a computer exchange of information. Problems are dealt with on a much more immediate basis. Much of the superficiality of the process of intellectual exchange is potentially eliminated by the nature of the medium.

Of equal importance is that individuals at all levels of experience have access to the system. Senior scholars and researchers, who may have more notoriety and influence because of what they have done in the past, rather than what they now are doing, are suddenly compelled to produce or to withdraw from the process of information exchange.

A computer networking system of the sort just suggested could be linked to major data bases, including bibliographical sources, data sets such as the census, or compilations of scientific information. Examples of such systems currently in operation cover a wide range of military, social service, educational, and scientific groups. The Electronic Information Exchange System, for example, is a networking system developed by Murray Turoff and funded during its initial phases by the National Science Foundation. Four different groups were set up using Turoff's system, including a group that was concerned with the research and development of devices for the disabled, a group of multidisciplinary researchers concerned with futurism, a group concerned with general systems theory, and a final group involved in research on social network systems. Message boards, conferencing capabilities, and notebook systems were made available to each of the four groups.[4]

Another example of this type of system in operation can be seen in the case of the conferencing system developed by Jacob Palme at the Swedish National Defense Research Institute. The system includes 375 active users, most of whom are researchers at various technical institutes throughout Sweden. Ten computers located throughout Sweden are used as the basis for the network. Cost to use the system is $7 to $14 per hour. Eighteen percent of the time spent on the system is conferencing. The remaining time is used by researchers either inputting data or retrieving it from the system.[5]

The Creation of Invisible Colleges and Universities

The importance of such systems of communication for the exchange of information and ideas cannot be overestimated. The successful pursuit of knowledge in almost any field of inquiry is dependent upon one's access to information sources. These include both documents and people. Through the linking of microcomputers and terminals to mainframe computers and communication systems (that is, the setting up of telematic systems), it is possible to create "invisible" or "electronic" colleges of scholars and researchers.

In such systems, it should be possible to approach research and the exchange of ideas in a manner and scope that have never been considered possible before. For the first time geographical location is not going to limit seriously what a scholar can or cannot do. As data bases expand and people with mutual interests become linked with one another by means of computer systems, it will be possible to pursue one's area of interest without too much difficulty. In areas such as the humanities where information is largely text oriented, books or manuscripts available only in a select series of libraries and research centers can be transmitted instantly to the most remote locations.

A plausible scenario, for example, is to put the collection

of the Library of Congress onto a computer memory system that could be drawn on by computer users across the country or even throughout the world. This is in fact being done as part of a pilot project for the Prints and Photographic Division of the Library of Congress, using video disks as the medium of storage. Thousands of graphic images included in the library's collection of caricatures and comic illustrations are stored on a single video disk. Works are organized in chronological order according to the individual artist. It is possible to review the holdings for a particular artist or to single out a particular work. Reviewing the materials included in the collection becomes much faster. Librarians do not have to pull materials except for more detailed examination by the researcher, collections are preserved as a result of being handled less, and materials can be effectively reviewed at any location across the country, provided the necessary disk and microcomputer equipment is available. While systems such as these are time consuming and expensive to develop, their actual cost in terms of the potential audience of users is extremely cheap. Essentially, for the first time it is possible to establish a truly national or even international research library that is not bound by the physical restraints of a library building.

The use of telematic systems makes possible the elimination of much of the traditional drudgery of research. Bibliographical work can be mechanized. Hand-done bibliograpical searchers that formerly took hundreds of hours of searching and copying can be completed in minutes, provided that the proper data bases and descriptors are employed. If the data generated from the search are transferred into the researcher's memory system, it is possible to develop massive bibliographies using a sophisticated text editor that can be inserted into ongoing research projects without even having to retype them. The increased productivity resulting from the use of such techniques could be astounding.

A scholar interested in a specialized area of research will find it possible to communicate directly with fellow researchers interested in the same subject. While one may argue fairly that this can already be done using the telephone and mail systems, the computer provides unprecedented advantages in terms of speed and the ability to generate, revise, and transmit printed documents.

Telematic Systems Create a New Paradigm for Conducting Research

The use of telematic systems in the development of research and scholarly networks represents a radical redefinition of how research and scholarship will be pursued in the future. Although solitary scholars will continue their work, collaborative efforts will be made more and more practical and desirable. Following Thomas Kuhn's arguments in *The Structure of Scientific Revolutions*, we will see a period in which researchers trained under the old system of scholarship will hold onto their methods and techniques of data collection and communication, while a new group of scholars and researchers will increasingly adopt the methods made possible by the introduction of telematic systems.[6]

Since the introduction of new methodological techniques implies the redefinition of power within any particular field, those who have been successful using the older system are likely to hold onto it as a means of maintaining their power and the status quo. The use of telematic systems, however, can so radically increase the productivity of the average scholar or researcher that not to use such methods will make it increasingly difficult or even impossible for those following the old methods of scholarship to compete.

A case in point can be seen in historical research. A scholar using telematic resources potentially has available online bibliographical systems, a high-speed text-oriented system for consulting with other researchers in the field, and a sophisticated text-editing or word-processing system with which to produce draft and final copies of manuscripts. In terms of the text-editing system alone, the researcher has available the services of an electronic "typist" who is as careful and precise as the researcher and is on call to do work at any time, day or night, throughout the entire year.

As the types of data available through online information systems expand, the resources open to the "telematic historian" will be even greater. Entire collections of rare books and documents, data bases such as U.S. Census compilations, as well as sophisticated analytical programs will redefine the standards of "good scholarship." Greater productivity and thoroughness in research will be demanded because such will be possible. Those with ability in their field, who also have a command of the new technology, will find themselves possessing a decided professional advantage.

The End of the Alexandrian Library

Daniel Bell has argued that the development of the new information systems will bring about the end of the traditional "Alexandrian Library." As he explains,

> The logic of all this is that the image of the Alexandrian Library—the single building like the Bibliotheque Nationale, the British Museum, or the Library of Congress —where all the world's recorded knowledge is housed in one building, may become a sad monument of the printed past. Data-based stores of information, especially in the scientific and technical field, will come from specialized information centers, transmitted through computer print-outs, facsimile, or video display to the user, who will have consulted an index through on-line searching to locate items of interest and then order them on demand.[7]

Books will not be made obsolete, however, because they are cheap and convenient.

Most specialized and technical information will be relegated to the computer banks rather than books or printed journals. Scholarly journals in almost every field will be available online as part of a computer data base, as they already are in many cases. Because of the high costs of typesetting, authors will often be required to submit manuscripts on magnetic storage systems in order to eliminate having to have the keyboarding for their articles done. Increasingly, books will also be produced this way. Soon, publishers will insist that a manuscript be capable of being "machine read" by a computer in one form or another.

The introduction of the new technology presents some decided problems and many exciting possibilities. Foremost among the problems is how to cope with the overwhelming amounts of information that are now made available by the new technology. The ability to carefully select what is relevant and irrelevant to one's work becomes more and more important. Among the most exciting possibilities is that individual researchers and scholars will be able increasingly to shape and control the content of their work to a much greater degree than has been possible up until now. For example, a humanities scholar using the current technology can typeset an entire book from the keyboard of a personal microcomputer. The completed text, with specialized type-setting commands embedded in it, can then be transmitted to a typesetter via a modem, at minimal cost. Particular care in the selection of the type, specialized printing, and graphic work can all be done at a greatly reduced cost. Smaller, more limited print runs will be affordable since the initial pro-duction of the book is cheaper. A "handcrafted" project becomes possible as a result of the introduction of the new electronic technology.

Implications of the New Technology for Scholarship

In 1972, the economist and futurist Robert Theobold commented:

> The intellectual magazines in this society, like *Harpers*, the *Atlantic*, the *New York Review of Books*, are still in the indus-trial era. There is no presently existing way of moving information about the world effectively. Those of us who

are trying to think about the new world cannot find each other and therefore cannot work together because we don't yet know how to communicate.[8]

The microcomputer revolution will redefine this situation completely. Totally new information networks of unprecedented scope are now possible. The ability to create and efficiently run telematic systems has changed the character of research and scholarship in almost every field of inquiry. The use of inexpensive computer systems in "real time" (i.e., as word processors, filing systems, and telecommunicating systems) will expand the scholar's and researcher's capacity not only to exchange information but also to store it. All that is essentially necessary is the capability of the individual to plug into a network system. As Nora and Minc explain,

> This phenomenon strikes squarely at the whole of economic, technical, scientific, and academic activity. The same is true for the small firm, which henceforth will be able to go to a specialized bank to find such and such a manufacturing process, and for the forecasting of a large company, which will have available all the data concerning the outlook for the economy. All of these data existed before the installation of data banks, but most of the time they were scattered, unmanageable and difficult to use. It is ease of access that creates the need.[9]

Whether in academics or business, two individuals, one of whom makes use of telematic systems while the other is content with limited data sets and technical support, will find themselves operating on very different levels.[10] Besides greater productivity, the individual taking advantage of telematic systems will in many instances have results that will reflect a greater degree of detail. This detail may redefine the substance of what is being studied or analyzed. One negative consequence may be the intensification of the tendency toward overspecialization already evident in our culture.

The transition process that will have to take place in the

coming years will be both painful and confusing. Marshall McLuhan, in his work, *Understanding Media*, illustrates this via the Greek myth of Cadmus:

> The Greek myth about the alphabet was that Cadmus, reputedly the king who introduced the phonetic letters into Greece, sowed the dragon's teeth, and they sprang up armed men. Like any other myth, this one encapsulates a prolonged process into a flashing insight. The alphabet meant power and authority and control of military structures at a distance. When combined with papyrus, the alphabet spelled the end of the stationary temple bureaucracies and the priestly monopolies of knowledge and power.[11]

Through the rapid expansion and development of telematic systems, there will be a radical restructuring of the organization of knowledge. A new type of scholar and researcher, using the microcomputer and the mainframe computer as powerful tools not only for the analysis but the organization of data, will emerge in post-typographic culture; and this scholar's methods and means of inquiry and communication will in large part be rooted in telematic systems.

6 · Microcomputers and Colonialism

The role played by print in instituting new patterns of culture is not unfamiliar. But one natural consequence of the specializing action of the new forms of knowledge was that all kinds of power took on a strongly centralist character.

Marshall McLuhan

N his essay, "The Information Society," Daniel Bell argues that, "just as capital and labor have been the central variables of industrial society, so information and knowledge are crucial variables of postindustrial society."[1] If Bell's argument is correct, then the control of knowledge will be the key to political and social power in the late twentieth and early twenty-first centuries.

Advanced technological cultures such as the United States have just begun to enter the postindustrial era. In doing so, traditional lines of power and authority have begun to be redefined. According to Feigenbaum and McCorduck, the world is entering a new period:

> The wealth of nations, which depended upon land, labor and capital during its agricultural and industrial phases— depended upon natural resources, the accumulation of money, and even upon weaponry—will come to depend in the future upon information, knowledge and intelligence.[2]

They explain that the traditional forms of material wealth will remain important but be superseded by the *control* of resources. Power will reside with those who have control of "facts, skills, codified experience, large amounts of easily obtained data, all accessible in fast, powerful ways to anybody who wants it."[3] More than in any time in our previous experience, knowledge and the control of information will be the basis of power.

During the period between 1500 and 1900, most of the world was under the political and economic control of Europe. Countries such as England, France, Germany, Holland, and Spain conquered native populations and took control of their physical wealth and resources. Material resources flowed into Europe from the colonies. Native languages and traditions were superseded by the European culture. Europe's technological superiority, including firearms, advanced shipbuilding, and sophisticated fortifications, provided the basis for its conquest of much of the world. In our own era, technology is responsible for fueling the colonial rivalries of the late twentieth century.

The parallels to the great European commercial rivalries of the sixteenth and seventeenth centuries are clear. As authors such as Feigenbaum and McCorduck have demonstrated, we are in the midst of a major struggle for technological supremacy and computer dominance with Japan.[4] It is a commercial rivalry as real as the one between England and Holland in the seventeenth century. The post-typographic or post-industrial culture that we are entering is just as dependent upon the computer and its ability to control information as the basis of social and economic power, as the English and the Dutch were dependent upon the importation of spices, rare woods, and other commodities from their colonial empires.

According to Feigenbaum and McCorduck, in post-industrial society "the computer is the knowledge worker's tool, as the planting and harvesting machines are to the farmer and the heavy industrial machines are to the manufacturing worker."[5] Presently, the United States dominates the world in computer technology. Obviously, from an economic point of view, this has been an enormous asset to the United States. Much of its future wealth will undoubtedly be based upon the growth and development of its computer industries. Significantly, however, the development of computer systems imply more than just the development of hardware, but also data banks and systems for the organization of knowledge. In this context, the United States is in an unusual position. Not only does it have the growing potential (Japan being its main competition) to dominate computer hardware, but software and data bases as well. While at first this may seem a trivial issue, it in fact represents what may be a significant form of cultural domination and imperialism.

The Computer and Cultural Imperialism

In the literature on educational theory with regard to developing nations, there has been an important analysis of education as a type of cultural imperialism. Authors such as Martin Carnoy, Philip G. Altbach, Gail P. Kelly, and others have outlined in detail how European imperial states imposed their cultural and educational values on subject colonies. History, language, and values derived from the metropolitan or imperial culture were considered superior and forced upon those under colonial rule. Native values and customs were considered inferior and ignored. Knowledge was based upon European values and norms, as was culture.[6]

Although the United States has not consciously tried to force its computer systems and technology on the world, its dominance and influence have inevitable cultural implications. Authors such as Nora and Minc have clearly argued that U.S. domination of computers and telematic systems is in fact a threat to other nations.[7] This is already true in television and satellite communications. As Daniel Bell explains,

> For France, the American domination of telecommunications and computers is a threat to its independence—in the crucially significant if not overriding area of technology and in the field of culture, where the American presence, through television and satellite, becomes an omnipresence.[8]

Bell's argument is a reasonable one. We currently dominate the production of broadcast media and also the distribution and launching of communication satellites through the space shuttle.

More important than media or communication satellites, however, is the fact that, more than any other country, the United States has the resources to organize large and extremely powerful general data banks (a process that it has already begun). These data banks will become even more important in the next few years. With the development of fifth-generation computers that will probably be in place by the early 1990s, automatic translation and interpretation will be practical.[9] In other words, we will see a world culture that for the first time, by means of telematics, will be speaking the same language, for all practical purposes.

Establishing the potential for a universal "electronic" language means that virtually any nation will be able to translate and take full advantage of American-developed data bases. It will be American data bases that are primarily used, since the United States has the most extensive resources available for their development. Nora and Minc quite reasonably predict that

> knowledge will end up by being shaped, as it always has been, by the available stock of information. Leaving to others—i.e., to American data banks—the responsibility for organizing this "collective memory" while being content to plumb it is to accept a form of cultural alienation. Installing data banks is an imperative of national sovereignty.[10]

The Naming of the Parts

The development of computer data banks such as the ones just described implies the restructuring of knowledge. New patterns will be established that are no longer rooted in traditional knowledge systems but in the particular architecture and organization of computers and telematic systems. Since criteria based upon American cultural models will prevail, the United States will have the potential to impose its organization and systems of knowledge upon other nations. A case in point can be seen in the development of descriptors and indexing systems.

In telematic systems the ability to retrieve a piece of information or data is based upon how it has been catalogued or indexed. If descriptors or classifications are not included in a system—or if they are inadequate to delineate the complexity of a subject—then they are essentially lost to the user. How the descriptors are defined in a certain sense defines not only the structure of available knowledge and information but also what can be known.

Such a fact puts those individuals not involved in the organization and definition of the knowledge system or data base at a decided disadvantage. We essentially learn and act upon what we have available to us in the way of information.

We cannot act upon or react to information that we cannot draw into our analytical framework or consciousness. If, as McLuhan argues, "all forms of wealth result from the movement of information,"[11] then the United States will have an extremely powerful incentive to control the organization and restrict the use of its data banks.

As was the case with colonial cultures, the future use of the languages of those societies dependent upon American data banks will be carefully circumscribed. Although, as argued earlier, there will probably be universal, computer-based translators and interpreters available by the early 1990s, the generation of new language forms will come from those controlling and creating the new software systems and data bases.

McLuhan recognized the importance of this issue, arguing that traditional language itself would be threatened by the new electric technology. According to him,

> Our new electric technology that extends our senses and nerves in a global embrace has large implications for the future of language. Electric technology does not need words any more than the digital computer needs numbers. Electricity points the way to an extension of the process of consciousness itself, on a world scale, and without any verbalization whatever.[12]

Just as the electronic visual images referred to by McLuhan will have the potential to supersede traditional language, so too is there the potential to create a new universal "electronic" language. Significantly, the new "electronic" language will be based upon the American way of organizing knowledge and consciousness.

"Newspeak"

There are numerous threats inherent in the "new intelligence" provided by computer and telematic systems. Because they operate most efficiently with their own special abbreviations and codes, it is likely that these codes and abbreviations will increasingly make their way into and possibly shape and control our language. What will happen to traditional writing, for example, when a computer-processed language, clear in substance but limited in meaning, invades our culture?

George Orwell's vision in *1984* of language being transformed into "Newspeak" (an abbreviated and propaganda-oriented language) is made increasingly possible and likely with computer and telematic systems. Combined with media such as television and radio, one wonders if the process may not in fact be inevitable.

The social and political implications of allowing the computer to shape and formulate language are profound. As Nora and Minc maintain,

> Language translates and generates a method of organization: to touch it is to shake society itself. In effect, it produces and reproduces the social hierarchy, certainly the speech of the lower classes is now more remote from that of the dominant classes than their respective lifestyles. Cultural inequality is by now predominant, and language plays a major role in it. Will the general adoption of processed language favor emancipation or will it emphasize the differences?[13]

Different classes will appropriate and employ language in different ways. Its mastery will represent a struggle for the control of culture.

Corporate Structures of Knowledge

One may well ask, even within the United States, who will determine the new organization and structure of knowledge. Clearly, this will not necessarily be the prerogative of the government or the universities, or other democratic institutions, but may by default become the exclusive domain of the corporations that develop the software systems and the data bases. Nora and Minc recognized this possibility when they argued that any policy established by France that attempts to counteract American computer and telematic domination also must

> take into account the renewal of the IBM challenge. Once a manufacturer of machines, soon to become a telecommunications administrator, IBM is following a strategy that will enable it to set up a communications network and to control it. When it does, it will encroach upon a traditional sphere of government power, communications. In the absence of a suitable policy, alliances will develop that involve the administrator of the network and the American data banks, to which it [IBM] will facilitate access.[14]

What is good for General Motors or IBM may not be good for the nation. While it would be unreasonable to suggest that a conspiracy is developing among corporate computer giants such as IBM and Digital Systems to seize control of the organization and dissemination of knowledge in our culture, it may very well be something that could happen by default.

Nora and Minc maintain that, for France, "only action by the authorities, standardizing the networks, launching communication satellites, and creating data banks, can give an original model for society with room to develop."[15] The same arguments would seem to apply for the United States and other countries as well. As the new electronic and telematic technology thrusts us in one direction, it may be extremely important for us to deliberately set ourselves on an opposing course. McLuhan argued, for example, that

> the implosion of electric energy in our century cannot be met by explosion or expansion, but it can be met by decentralism and the flexibility of multiple small centers. For example, the rush of students into our universities is not explosion but implosion. And the needful strategy to

encounter this force is not to enlarge the university, but to create numerous groups of autonomous colleges in place of our centralized university plant that grew up on the lines of European government and nineteenth-century industry.[16]

The development of multiple and independent data bases and telematic systems in general may be crucial in determining the freedom that will be afforded in our culture in the future.

In conclusion, as we have the potential through the new telematic systems to extend our consciousness through the whole of humankind, we must seriously consider the consequences of our action. Post-typographic culture has the potential to be enslaved by the computer or liberated by it. Ultimately we must make carefully considered judgments and provide safeguards that will insure their best use.

7 · Microcomputers and Education

Had the Schoolmen with their complex
oral culture understood the Gutenberg
technology, they could have created a new
synthesis of written and oral education,
instead of bowing out of the picture and
allowing the merely visual page to take
over the enterprise.

Marshall McLuhan

N this book I have attempted to demonstrate that we are at a turning point in our culture that comes as a result of the widespread proliferation and use of computers and microcomputers. In doing so, I have combined the subject matter of a number of disciplines. My outlook is that of a historian, social theorist, and, most important, an educator. Undoubtedly, many of my explanations have been far too general to please many computer specialists; however, addressing their concerns has not been my purpose. Instead, I have tried to establish a framework within which educators at all levels of the educational system, as well as those concerned with computers in general, can address some of the problems emerging in the computer-oriented culture that is developing around us.

I wish to begin this chapter by returning to a theme first introduced in the preface, namely, the question of how we can move beyond an image of man as machine (*l'homme machine*) to an image of human beings as meaning seekers and meaning makers (*homo poeta*). Like Ernest Becker, I believe that we create evil when we design structures or institutions that make it impossible for us as individuals to act productively and creatively.[1] Inherent in the possibilities provided by the emergence of a post-typographic culture are important new ways of organizing and controlling information and knowledge —ones that can affect our productivity and creativeness. The computer, and more specifically the microcomputer, is the key to this new system of information and knowledge. As the creators of this new system, we are morally obliged to ask whether or not we are setting in place, through our use of computers, social structures that will allow us to act in the best interests of our humanity. Or, are we instead creating conditions that will encourage computers and telematic systems to be used as tools of manipulation and domination?

Computer Literacy and Education

The most fundamental problem faced by educators in relation to computers is that of defining computer literacy.

This task is part of the much larger question of how and why we are using computers in our schools and society.

Establishing a usable definition of computer literacy is a difficult task. The computer is a universal machine. It is a framework into which different programs can be loaded and set in operation. Essentially, each program makes the computer into a new machine. The same equipment may be used to collect information for a data base, analyze quantitative data, communicate with another computer, process words, or write a program in any of a number of computer languages. Therefore, the question of defining computer literacy becomes one of determining the individual needs of students and the ways in which they are likely to use the machine.

In the introductory essay to his book, *The Computer in the School*, Robert Taylor argues that there are essentially three roles for the computer in education: (1) tutor, (2) tool, and (3) tutee. As tutor, the computer is used to lead students through drills and exercises where rote learning is necessary. This is of particular value in areas such as arithmetic or spelling, or at a more advanced level in subjects such as chemistry or physics. In this context the computer fulfills the role of teaching machine. As tool, the computer is used by the student as a word processor, a graphics design system, or as a manipulator of mathematical data. Significantly, it provides the means by which a person can work more creatively and efficiently. Finally, as tutee, the computer is programmed by the student. Through the manipulation of a computer language, a student literally instructs the computer to perform a specific set of operations or functions.[2]

Considerable controversy exists over how the computer can best be used in the process of instruction. Does computer literacy require that students be familiar with all three approaches outlined by Taylor? Are different uses of the computer best suited for different age groups? Joseph Weizenbaum, Professor of Computer Science at the Massachusetts Institute of Technology (MIT), argues that the whole notion of computer literacy is a delusion. Just because the world is increasingly pervaded by computers does not mean that everybody needs to be computer literate. Drawing an analogy between computers and electric motors, Weizen-baum argues that, while almost everybody owns a lot of electric motors (in automobiles, clocks, vacuum cleaners, refrigerators, and so forth), electric motor literacy is not required to use these devices. Most electric motors are so widely in use that they are not thought of as motors but are simply taken for granted and used. For all practical purposes their existence is ignored by their users.[3]

In much the same way, according to Weizenbaum, the computer will become largely invisible. Worrying about whether or not an individual is computer literate will become largely unnecessary. Small, specialized computers already tell us the time, indicate when we have left the door of our cars open, and tune in our favorite television and radio stations. Larger machines that we think of more specifically as being "computers" are already rapidly evolving to such a point that they can be used for sophisticated purposes with little or no introduction. An example of this can be seen in the case of the Apple Macintosh computer, which allows a user to do word processing and sophisticated graphics with minimal instruction.

Weizenbaum assumes that teaching children computer languages and how to program computers is unnecessary. While as a technically oriented society we need computer programmers, most people using computers do not need to know how to program. Instead they need to be able to run application programs that fit their specific needs. According to Weizenbaum, the emphasis on having children learn computer languages is misplaced:

> It is clear to me that computer languages are not like natural languages. I think they are more like mathematical languages or physics. They require a certain intellectual maturity, you can learn them relatively quickly. It isn't worth spending a lot of time on at an early age.[4]

Weizenbaum goes on to maintain that

> the introduction of computers into primary and secondary schools is basically a mistake based on very false assump-

tions about computers. Our schools are already in desperate trouble and the introduction of the computer at this time is, at very best, a diversion—possibly a dangerous diversion.[5]

He is opposed to the computer being used as a quick technological fix for education. He believes that its potential as tool, tutor, or tutee is grossly overestimated and used in misleading ways.

LOGO: To Understand Is to Invent

Weizenbaum's rejection of the use of the computer as an important pedagogical tool is contradicted, at least in part, by his colleague at MIT, Seymour Papert, who has been largely responsible for the development of the computer language, LOGO. In his discussion of LOGO, Papert does not deal with the use of the computer in terms of multiple categories as did Taylor. Instead, he focuses on the issue of programming—specifically, whether the child is being programmed by the computer or the child is programming the computer. According to him, in many schools today, the phrase

> "computer-aided instruction" means making the computer teach the child. One might say the *computer is being used to program* the child. In my vision, *the child programs the computer* and in doing so, both acquires a sense of mastery over a piece of the most modern and powerful technology and establishes an intimate contact with some of the deepest ideas from science, from mathematics, and from the art of intellectual model building.[6]

If microcomputers are used in the school simply to provide "computer-aided instruction" (as "tutors," using Taylor's classification), their interest and appeal, according to Papert, are likely to remain relatively limited. According to Papert, the real significance of the computer as an instructional tool lies in its use as a means of extending the user's intelligence. Through the use of the computer, students are able to deal with complex problems. Statistical analyses are no longer limited to simplified calculations, and the scale of simulations is infinitely greater. Curricula can be personally developed for each student, so the division of students into grade levels will have less meaning.[7]

Papert argues that the computer not only has the potential to enhance the thinking process of the learner but also to change the patterns of access to knowledge. He believes that

> computers can be carriers of powerful ideas and of the seeds of cultural change, . . . they can help people form new relationships with knowledge that cuts across the traditional lines separating humanities from science and knowledge of the self from both of these.[8]

According to Papert, it is in its ability to bring together traditionally disparate fields that the present computer revolution has its greatest positive potential for creating change and redefining the meaning of knowledge in our culture. For the first time, it may be possible to supersede the separation and division of knowledge based upon the traditional disciplines.

Papert has depended heavily on the work of the Swiss psychologist Jean Piaget in formulating his method of educating children through the use of computers. Like Piaget, he assumes that the child is a "builder" of ideas, structuring reality.[9] This perception is directly related to Piaget's conviction that "to understand is to invent."[10] According to Piaget, the functions of intelligence consist of understanding and inventing and of building up structures by structuring reality.

For Papert, the computer, and in particular the microcomputer, provide the child with the ultimate tool with which to begin to structure reality. Significantly, what is learned through the computer has the potential to take root outside of the context of the computer. For him, the computer is a "*carrier* of cultural "germs" or "seeds" whose intellectual products will not need technological support once they take root in any actively growing mind."[11]

Papert carefully distinguishes how teaching a child to program in a computer language such as LOGO differs significantly from how other technologies such as television and printing affect the learning process. According to Papert, in contrast to a child reading a book or watching a program such as "Sesame Street,"

> when a child learns to program, the process of learning is transformed. It becomes more active and self-directed. In particular, the knowledge is acquired for a recognizable personal purpose. The child does something with it. The new knowledge is a source of power and is experienced as such from the moment it begins to form in the child's mind.[12]

In programming the computer (having it function as a tutee, according to Taylor), the child learns not so much whether a certain approach to formulating a program is right or wrong, but instead how it can be fixed. The object of intellectual inquiry is not simply to get the right answer to a question but to understand how a structure or idea is put together, how it functions, and how it can be improved upon. By means such as these, the child is introduced to a process of intellectual inquiry that, according to Papert, almost exactly reproduces that of the adult inquirer.

Papert's proposal to introduce LOGO as a major part of the curriculum of the schools is appealing on the surface but may in fact, by itself, have a dehumanizing effect on children. Having them learn to program in a language such as LOGO is undoubtedly useful in many respects, but whether or not children learn to think better and more creatively as a result of learning LOGO, and whether or not the skills acquired through its use are transferable, are questions that will require further research. No matter what the answers to these questions are, LOGO remains limited because it is child centered rather than subject centered. Essentially it eliminates subject and substitutes in its place method or technique.

Over three decades ago the French social theorist Jacques Ellul formulated one of the most comprehensive and forceful critiques of technological society ever written. In his work, *The Technological Society*, he argued that we live in a progressively technical civilization in which *technique* increasingly dominates our day-to-day lives. In doing so we are provided with a set of standardized means for achieving a set of predetermined results. According to Ellul,

> *Technique* is the *totality of methods rationally arrived at and having absolute efficiency* (for a given stage of development) in *every* field of human activity. Its characteristics are new; the technique of the present has no common measure with that of the past.[13]

LOGO as a computer language is a rationalized behavior —one that reduces education and learning to the method or technique of computer programming. In doing so, according to Robert Sardello, it assumes that it is "truly a language— not a constructed, artificial language, but a language fully capable of expressing the full and complete life of a people."[14] Such a task is beyond the limited capacity of an artificial language such as LOGO. What is even more disturbing is that "it assumes that language no longer emanates from the life of a community, from geographical place, from heritage, ritual, from the living body of a people, from the voice of things in the world."[15] While the microworld proposed by Papert is interesting and certainly worth exploring, one cannot help but feel that it is also an impoverished world, one largely reflecting *technique* rather than substance. Taken by itself the microworld created by LOGO is an inadequate environment in which to have the child grow and develop. Moreover, while the use of a language like LOGO can contribute to the definition of computer literacy, in and of itself, it cannot provide a foundation for computer literacy.

Computer Literacy in a Post-Typographic Culture

Computer literacy, if it is to be meaningful, must be defined in terms of the needs of the culture that is emerging around us, and in terms of the needs of the individuals who are a part of that culture. The skills demanded by a post-typographic culture, as described in the earlier part of this book, fall into two domains: The first involves providing the individual with the necessary skills to access, manipulate, and control information. The computer as a universal machine can free our imaginations, not only by expanding the sources of information available to us, but also by making them enormously more efficient. The second domain involves understanding the limitations and potential threat to freedom and action that can occur if the computer is inappropriately used. Keeping Taylor's categories in mind, computer literacy in a post-typographic culture should focus primarily on the use of the computer as a tool. The use of the computer as a tutor for computer-assisted instruction does not pose a real threat to the integrity of the educational system and the culture. The only problem is that, unless the computer-assisted instruction is of extremely high quality and used creatively, the job may be more efficiently and cheaply done through use of the traditional curricular materials and instruction. Finally, the use of the computer as a tutee in the form of programming in languages such as LOGO may be appropriate as a supplemental part of the curriculum, but it should not represent its primary thrust.

What is clearly needed is a much more carefully defined set of objectives concerning how and why we are using computers in conjunction with the schools. Computer literacy, if it is to be meaningful, must also move beyond the use of the machine merely as a tool and take into account the moral, ethical, and social issues implicit in the use of the new technology. Students must be made aware of the potential of the computer as a tool to dominate and control, as well as to liberate and enlighten. While some may argue that my definition of computer literacy is simplistic, I would maintain that its simplicity nonetheless meets the demands imposed by the post-typographic culture that is emerging around us. Computer literacy ultimately demands that we provide each individual with the means (1) to use the computer as a tool in a way that is appropriate to the context in which each person lives and works and (2) to understand the moral, ethical, and social implications underlying the use of computers within the larger culture and society of which each person is a part.

Deus ex Machina

In a time of intense criticism of the public school system in the United States, the computer has been looked to by many people as a cure for many of the problems that currently face us in education. In fact, along with its many possibilities, the computer introduces a whole new series of problems.

School systems, from the level of the superintendent through the individual classroom instructor, are faced with intense pressure from parents, the business community, and political officials to make students computer literate. Yet none of these groups seems to have a very clear understanding of what they mean by being computer literate, or the cultural and social implications underlying their confused demands for literacy.

The temptation on the part of school officials to jump on the computer bandwagon is overwhelming. Reputations and careers are to be made by educators promoting this latest and most current educational innovation. Pushing computers in the schools is where the money is.[16] No one wants to be labeled old-fashioned or out of the mainstream. Similar sentiments led to the widespread adoption of innovations during the 1960s such as the "new math" and open-construction classrooms.

Unlike these innovations, however, which were confined to within the schools, the computer and microcomputer revolution has a foundation of support that exists within the larger culture. The promotion of computer literacy in the schools is of enormous potential benefit to computer manufacturers such as IBM and Apple Computer. It was no accident that Apple Computer's chairman, Steven Jobs, with the help of U.S. Representative Fortney H. Stark of California's 9th District, attempted to pass a bill in Congress in

1982 that would provide tax incentives sufficient to allow Apple to donate, at virtually no cost, a computer to every elementary and secondary school in the United States. Other computer companies followed Job's initiative by having similar proposals introduced. Job's bill, which would have cost the Treasury $300 million in revenue, was quickly approved by House and Senate subcommittees and was approved by the House of Representatives by a margin of 323 to 62 votes. Only the adjournment of the 97th Congress before the Senate could consider the bill prevented its final passage.[17]

As Douglas Sloan has so aptly explained,

> It does not take a flaming Bolshevik, nor even a benighted neo-Luddite, to wonder whether all those computer companies, and their related textbook publishers, that are mounting media campaigns for computer literacy and supplying hundreds of thousands of computers to schools and colleges really have the interests of children and young people as their primary concern.[18]

Education in a Post-Typographic Culture

The implications for education underlying the widespread introduction and use of computers into our culture are staggering. Traditional learning will be redefined. Our definitions of what constitutes an educated person will no longer be the same. The retention of factual information will no longer be as important as the ability to access information.

> Discrimination will then be based less on the storage of knowledge than the ability to research and use it. Concepts will prevail over facts, iteration over recitation. Accepting this transformation will constitute a Copernican revolution for pedagogy.[19]

Traditional schooling, unless it is linked to the new knowledge systems that are emerging, is likely to become less and less relevant to the majority of students. A cultural lag will exist between what it is possible to know through the new data banks and what it is possible to know through what is taught in the schools. Unless the curriculum of the schools is adapted to the emerging structures of knowledge provided by the computer, they may function more as custodial institutions than as institutions of learning.

Some would argue that to some extent this has already happened as a result of the introduction of television. Since television first became commercially available in the late 1940s, students and the general population have increasingly depended upon it as the source of much of their general information and knowledge. General information that in the past was communicated through the schools or printed sources can now be learned from television. Significantly, by its very nature (although this is changing with the introduction of specialized cable channels), television does not provide the viewer with the opportunity to select, except in the most general way, what it is that he or she is going to learn about. Also, the type of knowledge best communicated by television is of a highly generalized, unfocused nature.

Although the schools have found it difficult to compete with the general information provided by television, they have to a large extent been able to maintain their control over specialized and focused knowledge. With the widespread introduction of affordable microcomputers and telematic systems, however, the schools have also begun to lose their control over the specialized knowledge and information that was largely their domain up until this time. Unless the schools adapt the new computer technology in exciting and meaningful ways into their structure and organization, their relevance to students at all levels—from slow and uninterested to gifted and highly motivated—will continue to diminish. Once again, the parallel with the introduction of printing and the typographical revolution of the late fifteenth and early sixteenth centuries is relevant. As Marshall McLuhan explained,

> Had the Schoolmen with their complex oral culture
> understood the Gutenberg technology, they could have

created a new synthesis of written and oral education, instead of bowing out of the picture and allowing the merely visual page to take over the educational enterprise. The Oral Schoolmen did not meet the new visual challenge of print, and the resulting expansion or explosion of Gutenberg technology was in many respects an impoverishment of the culture.[20]

As we begin to enter post-typographic culture, contemporary educators, from the elementary schools to the universities, are faced with a crisis essentially the same as the one faced by their scholastic predecessors nearly 500 years ago. The key question facing the educational system in the immediate future will be how it should redefine the structure and content of curricula to meet the demands and needs of a post-typographic culture, including educating children to be computer literate in a meaningful way.

The Two Cultures

Ideally, the computer has the potential to unify increasingly not only traditionally separated fields of knowledge but the educational system in general. C. P. Snow in his classic essay, *The Two Cultures and the Scientific Revolution*, argues quite convincingly that there exists an increasing polarization of intellectual life in Western society:

> At one pole we have the literary intellectuals, . . . at the other scientists, and as the most representative, the physical scientists. Between the two a gulf of mutual incomprehension—sometimes (particularly among the young) hostility and dislike, but most of all lack of understanding.[21]

According to Snow, neither the scientific culture nor the literary intellectuals talk to one another.[22] Snow tends to lay the blame for this lack of communication on those following the literary rather than the scientific traditions. Yet, in fact, the differences between the two groups may not be as great as many people assume, but instead may lie in the "language" systems they employ.

Initially, for example, the types of questions pursued by a historian and those with which a physicist is concerned may appear to hold very little in common. If we reduce the research each is pursuing down to its essential questions, however, we find that they are asking many of the same things. Both the historian and the scientist are asking questions related to cause and effect, both generate hypotheses, and both are concerned about the influence of their point of view on their interpretation of data.

Different areas of intellectual inquiry have tended to develop language systems exclusively for their own use. For better or worse, the computer and telematic systems imply the ordering and structuring of knowledge along relatively well-defined and universal lines. Thus the programming of a computer by both the historian and the physicist will require identical or at least closely related language systems. While the knowledge they are interested in pursuing may be very different, the methods they use to process data (i.e., the computer and the language and logic systems employed with it) may be based on many of the same assumptions. Through their common access to a wider range of data sources and as a result of their sharing in the languages and means that allow both access to and manipulation of the computer, there is the possibility of drawing closer together the hitherto disparate scientific and literary intellectual traditions represented by these two types of scholars.

Ideally, there will be increasing crossover among scholarly fields. Traditional definitions of intellectual fields will become less rigid and circumscribed. Multiple models will emerge as data banks and access to them expand. As Nora and Minc explain,

> Data processing runs the risk of being at the source of one
> of those discontinuities around which knowledge revolves.
> The boundaries of disciplines will be more fluid, more
> mobile, because they will be the result of multiple

codifications, of scattered endeavours without direction or design. Related primarily to the nature of data banks, this evolution will thus reflect the influence of American culture, which is not organized into battle corps and does not establish guilds. The multiplication of configurations will reduce the importance of unifying classifications; knowledge will then lose the comforting support of a tradition and of a sociology. Will it gain an ounce of freedom from it?[23]

It is hoped that the answer to Nora's and Minc's question is yes. If the conflict between the traditional scientific culture and the literary intellectual tradition is reduced—that is, if each domain comes to understand the other somewhat better by sharing the common "language" system or structure of the computer—then the implications for education are extremely important.[24]

Ideally, ways of knowing rather than what is known will take precedence in the educational system. According to Nora and Minc,

Information that only teaches technical solutions, that lists facts without putting them into a perspective and without structuring them into a coherent project, and, on the other hand, information that proclaims ideals without inserting them into the practical development of society will increasingly be regarded as pseudo-information.[25]

New types of curricula and teacher training programs, and, ultimately, new types of teachers will have to emerge. Not only will the obvious skills of computer literacy be required of teachers, but also the ability to see their fields and the process of instruction in a way that transcends the rigid structure of traditional disciplines.

Microcomputers and Social Equality

In a society in which computer literacy will be an essential requirement for individuals to function, the access they have to both instruction and to the use of computers will be critical. Microcomputers are expensive and relatively complex tools. They are more readily available to the rich than the poor. We must be aware of how their availability can perpetuate existing patterns of racial, sexual, and social inequality.

To begin with, it is crucial that the computer become as universal throughout schools as textbooks. With the rapid lowering of the cost of microcomputers that has taken place in the past few years, this may in fact be possible. But access to computers alone may not be sufficient. In addition to proper basic instruction in computer use, access to online information systems and to sophisticated instructional programming will have to be available to anyone being educated in the society. Not to provide such access will ultimately represent a very real type of discrimination.

All sorts of complications arise. Those parents who are already familiar with computers and programming will undoubtedly push the hardest to make sure that their children are instructed in computer use. Students whose parents and siblings are computer literate and who are raised in a household where a computer is present will undoubtedly have a considerable advantage. Just as there is the process of "reading readiness" in which children are provided basic skills and background that helps them get into the process of reading, so too will there be the process of "computer readiness."

Once machines are in place in the schools, the next question is who will get access to them. Traditionally, women have been discouraged from pursuing mathematics as a serious field of study. As a result, the necessary mathematical foundation required for many advanced fields is not held by most women, so the professional opportunities that are open to them are more limited. One need only go into most elementary and secondary school computer facilities to see that the boys, conditioned to be more socially aggressive and assertive, tend to take control of the limited number of computers available, while the girls are encouraged to take their interests elsewhere. If access to the machines proves to be a crucial element in the ultimate development of adult intellectual and technical skills, then equal access to computers and telematic systems for everyone, regardless of socioeconomic status or sex, is crucial.

The Question of Continuous Education

It is increasingly clear that the microcomputer and telematic systems have the potential to act as catalysts for the redefinition of traditional modes of education. One would like to assume, as Nora and Minc do, that,

> in an ideal world of fully informed "wise men," organization would coincide with spontaneity: a perfect market society, in which education and information would make each person conscious of the collective constraints, and a fully planned society, in which the center would receive from each unit at the base correct messages concerning its order of preferences and would have the same structure and the same attitude. Information and participation advance together.[26]

Such ideals, however, do not conform with some of the realities that are beginning to emerge. A case in point can be seen in Adam Schaff's essay, "Occupation Versus Work," included in the recent Club of Rome report, *Microelectronics and Society*. Schaff argues persuasively, as do many other authors, that, as the microelectronic revolution advances, it will undoubtedly bring with it less and less need for traditional workers. To a large extent, traditional labor will be superfluous, and it will be necessary to find alternative activities for much of the population.[27] In Huxley's *Brave New World*, essentially the same problem was faced and dealt with by organizing a highly complex "leisure" culture in which people were encouraged to consume largely useless commodities and to participate in highly complex and time-consuming social and athletic activities.

Schaff suggests the process of continuous education as an alternative. According to him, as productivity increases it will be possible to shorten the number of working hours required of most people. This, however, would still result in a large number of people remaining unemployed. An alternative to unemployment would require adult learners to take part in compulsory education:

> The requirement for continuous education would be made realistic by the fact that people who are now regarded as structurally unemployed would receive from society means of subsistence at the level of needs shaped in the process of history. Society would thus be entitled to demand of them, as part of their responsibility to it, certain reciprocal performances, which would be made obligatory —during a period of life—for all.[28]

The possibilities of such a system are chilling. Schaff argues that the new system of education that would emerge would necessarily lead to the modification of the entire school system.[29] The potential for cultural and political indoctrination and the misuse of the school system as a giant custodial system for controlling the unemployed is enormous. Yet, if educators and those learning to use the computer are made aware of its potential threat to personal freedom, such a scenario becomes unlikely. Computer literacy, as defined in the earlier part of this chapter, becomes not only a tool through which to organize and collect information but also provides the critical insight and understanding necessary to maintain one's personal freedom and the traditional rights implicit in a democratic society.

Significance of the Computer's Presence for Education

The computer's presence has undeniable significance for education. Advancements in computer technology will lead to unprecedented changes in the traditional meaning of knowledge, as well as in the structure and content of the curriculum. As is the case in almost all its other applications, the new computer technology can provide the foundation for a Renaissance in our educational system or it can dehumanize it.

The decision as to which end will be realized is ultimately dependent not so much upon the technologies and innovations themselves—these are already in place—but on how we use them to structure information and access knowledge in our society. It is up to the schools to educate future generations to be computer literate. Computer literacy must encompass not only technical but also social and moral perspectives. As post-typographic culture becomes more defined, we must adapt our educational system to the demands of the new technology while at the same time sacrificing nothing of our humanity.

8 • Conclusion: Proteus and the Future of Intelligence

Appropriate technology reminds us that before we choose our tools and techniques we must choose our dreams and values, for some technologies serve them, while others make them unobtainable.

Tom Bender

HROUGHOUT history, the introduction of new technologies has brought with it social change. The invention of movable type and printing in the fifteenth century was responsible for creating not only an intellectual revolution but a political and cultural one as well. According to Marshall McLuhan,

> The role played by print in instituting new patterns of culture is not unfamiliar. But one natural consequence of the specializing forms of the new knowledge was that all kinds of power took on a strongly centralist character. Whereas the role of the feudal monarch had been inclusive, the king actually including in himself all his subjects, the Renaissance prince tended to become an exclusive power centre, surrounded by his individual subjects.[1]

In the English Industrial Revolution, a new class of political and social elites was empowered as a result of its control of the new motive force of the steam engine. In our own era, the computer revolution promises to be a force of equal magnitude.

The mutable and changing character of the computer makes it difficult to anticipate what type of culture and society the new technology is likely to create. An analogy with the ancient Greek sea god, Proteus, comes to mind. If one could capture and hold on to Proteus, he would grant his captor whatever he or she wanted. The only problem was that Proteus could change his shape or form at will. One might capture the god in the form of a man, but he would transform himself into a snake or a lion or even a mouse. Each time his captor would grasp him, he would change into yet another form and confuse any who would hold him as a prisoner.

Like Proteus, the computer and telematic systems are mutable and changing, constantly redefining themselves as we advance farther and farther into a post-typographic culture. At the same time, they are redefining our under-

standing of the world we live in and our traditional definitions of knowledge and intelligence.

New Conceptions of Knowledge and Intelligence

Clearly the nature of knowledge and the meaning of
intelligence are no longer the same in a post-typographic
culture as they were in a typographic culture. In the past, to
be intelligent required the ability to solve difficult problems
by organizing information, ideas, and thoughts. As Marvin
Minsky argues,

> An expert solves problems that others think hard with
> little time or apparent effort. Common sense says that this
> must be because he "knows how to solve them." In this
> sense, being intelligent is not an activity of the moment;
> one must have accumulated, perhaps over a span of years,
> the knowledge (procedures) needed for the performance.
> And to do that, in turn, one must have learned to use the
> mechanisms for acquiring that knowledge.[2]

In years to come, one's intelligence will increasingly come to
be judged by one's ability to merge one's thoughts with the
information and data provided by the computer.

We are faced with a new dimension in our definition of
knowledge and intelligence. As the harnessing of energy was
the necessary condition for the creation of an industrial
society, the harnessing of the computer both as a technology
and as a moral force is the necessary condition of post-
typographic culture. We are at a moment in history when the
Gutenberg Galaxy of the past 500 years is being superseded
by a new post-typographic culture. The conflicts inherent in
the redefinition of knowledge and culture that will result are
inevitable. McLuhan stated it this way:

> What will be the new configurations of mechanisms and
> of literacy as these older forms of perception and judg-

ment are interpenetrated by the new electric age? The new electric galaxy of events has already moved deeply into the Gutenberg galaxy. Even without collision, such co-existence of technologies and awareness brings traumas and tension to every living person. Our most ordinary and conventional attitudes seem suddenly twisted into gargoyles and grotesques.[3]

Already it is clear that by redefining our ability to organize information and manipulate ideas, the computer has made our traditional definitions of education and knowledge no longer sufficient.

The widespread use of the computer as a means by which to organize and control knowledge—to maximize human intelligence—is as important a revolution in the history of thought and thinking as the invention of writing or the Gutenberg revolution with its invention of movable type. McLuhan commented:

> As the Sumerians were writing the first hieroglyphs on wax tablets, they were living, probably without realizing it, through a decisive change for mankind: the appearance of writing. At the present time, data processing is perhaps introducing a comparable phenomenon. The analogies are striking: extension of memory; proliferation and changes in information systems; possibly a change in the models of authority.[4]

Cybernetics and Post-Typographic Culture

The mathematician Norbert Weiner spent the final years of his life trying to address the question of how people would cope with the new technologies that were emerging and reshaping both science and society. In the years between the end of the Second World War and his death in the early 1960s, he evolved a theory of control and communication in the animal and the machine that he eventually defined in a single term, *cybernetics.*[5]

Weiner derived the term *cybernetics* from the Greek word *kubernetes*, or "steersman."[6] There is a certain irony in his choice of words, for it is ultimately the question of how we will employ the extraordinary potential of the new cybernetic systems—what course or direction we will steer—that will determine the nature of post-typographic culture.

The task before us is a difficult one. We are at a rare moment in history in which we are able to observe a process of intellectual and social transformation with few and perhaps no precedents in human experience. As we enter the new post-typographic era, we must remember that, although human beings are tool makers and machine builders (*homo faber*), they are also dream makers. Post-typographic culture is a creation of the new technology. Men and women are its potential masters. It is their choice whether they allow the new technology to rule them or whether they use it instead to realize their dreams.

Notes

Preface

1. Ernest Becker, *The Structure of Evil: An Essay on the Unification of the Science of Man* (New York: George Braziller, 1968). Becker's main discussion of *homo poeta* is found on pages 169–76.

Chapter 1. The Emergence of Post-Typographic Culture

1. Marshall McLuhan, *The Gutenberg Galaxy: The Making of Typographic Man* (Toronto: University of Toronto Press, 1962).

2. Marshall McLuhan, *Understanding Media: The Extensions of Man* (New York: Mentor Books, 1964).

3. Arthur C. Clarke, *Profiles of the Future: An Inquiry into the Limits of the Possible* (New York: Popular Library, 1977), p. 233.

4. McLuhan, *Understanding Media*, p. iv.

5. Ibid.

6. Ibid.

7. Edward A. Feigenbaum and Pamela McCorduck, *The Fifth Generation: Artificial Intelligence and Japan's Computer Challenge to the World* (Reading, Mass.: Addison-Wesley, 1983), pp. 18–19.

8. Ibid., p. 19.

9. Lucien Febvre and Henri-Jean Martin, *The Coming of the Book: The Impact of Printing, 1450–1800*, trans. David Gerard (London: NLB, 1976), p. 10. Febvre and Martin's book, although a classic, has recently been superseded by Elizabeth L. Eisenstein's

two-volume work, *The Printing Press as an Agent of Change: Communications and Cultural Transformations in Early-Modern Europe* (Cambridge: Cambridge University Press, 1979).

10. McLuhan, *Understanding Media*, pp. 64, 65.

11. Ibid., p. 64.

12. Marcel Thomas, "Manuscripts," in Febvre and Martin, *The Coming of the Book*, p. 15.

13. Henri-Jean Martin, "Printing," in Raymond Williams, ed., *Contact: Human Communication and Its History* (New York: Thames and Hudson, 1981), p. 131.

14. Thomas, "Manuscripts," p. 17.

15. Ibid., p. 19.

16. Ibid., p. 20.

17. Harold A. Innis, *Empire and Communication* (Oxford: Oxford University Press, 1950), p. 141.

18. Literacy was sufficiently widespread in Europe by the beginning of the fifteenth century that the clergy probably represented a minority of those people who could read and write. Of course, at what level people were literate poses an entirely different type of issue. See John Carter and Percy H. Muir, eds., *Printing and the Mind of Man* (New York: Holt, Rinehart and Winston, 1967), p. xviii.

19. Ibid., pp. 146–47.

20. Febvre and Martin, *The Coming of the Book*, p. 248.

21. Ibid., p. 249.

22. Ibid., p. 207.

23. Ibid., p. 294.

Chapter 2. The Information Society

1. Christopher Evans, *The Making of the Micro: A History of the Computer* (New York: Van Nostrand Reinhold, 1981), p. 13.

2. Quoted in Christopher Evans, *The Micro Millennium* (New York: Viking Press, 1979), p. 27.

3. Quoted in Jeremy Bernstein, *The Analytical Engine: Computers —Past, Present and Future* (New York: Random House, 1978), p. 38.

4. Charles Eames and Ray Eames, *A Computer Perspective*, ed. Glen Fleck, (Cambridge, Mass.: Harvard University Press, 1973), pp. 23–25, 132–33.

5. Evans, *The Micro Millennium*, p. 76.

6. Evans, *The Making of the Micro*, p. 104.

7. Bernstein, *The Analytical Engine*, p. 76.

8. Seymour Papert, *Mindstorms: Children, Computers and Power Ideas* (New York: Basic Books, 1980), p. 24.

9. Daniel Bell, *The Coming of Post-Industrial Society: A Venture in Social Forecasting* (New York: Basic Books, 1973).

10. Daniel Bell, "The Social Framework of the Information Society" in Michael L. Dertouzos and Joel Moses, eds., *The Computer Age: A Twenty-Year View* (Cambridge, Mass.: MIT Press, 1979), p. 164.

11. Ibid., p. 168.

12. Ibid., p. 163.

13. C. L. Becker, *Progress and Power* (Stanford, Calif.: Stanford University Press, 1936).

14. Norbert Weiner, *The Human Use of Human Beings: Cybernetics and Society* (New York: Avon Books, 1967). Originally published in 1950.

15. Harold A. Innis, *Empire and Communication* (Oxford: Oxford University Press, 1950), p. 7.

16. Wiener, *Cybernetics and Society*, p. 26.

17. Marshall McLuhan, *The Gutenberg Galaxy: The Making of Typographic Man* (Toronto: University of Toronto Press, 1962), p. 278.

18. Bell, "The Social Framework of the Information Society."

19. McLuhan, *The Gutenberg Galaxy*, pp. 278–79.

20. Douglas Sloan, "Introduction: On Raising Critical Questions About the Computer in Education," in Douglas Sloan, ed., *The Computer in Education: A Critical Perspective* (New York: Teachers College Press, 1985), p. 1.

21. Ibid., p. 3.

Chapter 3. Microcomputers and Telematic Consciousness

1. Simon Nora and Alain Minc, *The Computerization of Society: A Report to the President of France* (Cambridge: Mass.: MIT Press, 1980), p. 3.

2. DIALOG Information Services, Inc., "Worldwide Information on Command" (Palo Alto, Calif.: DIALOG Information Services, 1982), n.p.

3. Ibid.

4. Nora and Minc, *The Computerization of Society*, p. 3.

5. Ibid., p. 5.

6. DIALOG, for example, currently includes among its data bases CLAIMStm/CHEM; CLAIMStm/CITATION; CLAIMStm/CLASS; CLAIMStm/UNITERM; CLAIMStm/U.S. PATENTS; CLAIMStm/U.S. PATENT ABSTRACTS; CLAIMStm/U.S. PATENT ABSTRACTS WEEKLY.

7. Nora and Minc, *The Computerization of Society*, p. 52.

8. Ibid.

9. Ibid., p. 53.

10. David Burnham, *The Rise of the Computer State* (New York: Random House, 1983). See in particular Burnham's concluding chapter "A Future," pp. 226–58.

11. Ibid., p. 10.

12. Ibid.

13. Ibid., p. 13.

14. Nora and Minc, *The Computerization of Society*, p. 59.

15. Ibid., p. 132.

16. Douglas Sloan, "Introduction: On Raising Critical Questions About the Computer in Education," in Douglas Sloan, ed., *The Computer in Education: A Critical Perspective* (New York: Teachers College Press, 1985), p. 2.

Chapter 4. Microcomputers and the Neo-Luddites

1. Arthur C. Clarke, *2001: A Space Odyssey* (New York: New American Library, 1968). Also see Clarke's *2010: Space Odyssey Two* (New York: Ballantine Books, 1982), where the history of the HAL 9000 series computer is outlined in detail.

2. Mary Wollstonecraft Shelley, *Frankenstein, or, the Modern Prometheus* (Indianapolis: Bobbs-Merrill, 1974).

3. Malcolm I. Thomis, *The Luddites: Machine-Breaking in Regency England* (Hamden, Conn.: Archon Books, 1970), p. 14.

4. Ibid., p. 12.

5. Ibid., p. 11.

6. Ibid., p. 14. Significantly, Thomis argues that the Luddites' opposition to machines did not imply any particular hostility to machinery as such, but instead to larger social and economic issues. The machines themselves were "just a conveniently exposed target against which an attack could be made."

7. Simon Nora and Alain Minc, *The Computerization of Society: A*

Report to the President of France (Cambridge: Mass.: MIT Press, 1980), p. 10.

8. Ibid.

9. Ibid.

10. Ibid., p. 11.

11. Ibid.

12. Ibid., p. 133.

13. Ibid., p. 134.

14. Aldous Huxley, *Brave New World* (New York: Harper & Row, 1969); George Orwell, *1984* (New York: Signet Library, 1961).

15. Samuel Butler, *Erewhon* (New York: Airmont, 1967).

16. Ibid., p. 12.

17. Ibid., p. 144.

18. Ibid., p. 146.

19. Ibid., p. 148.

20. Ibid., p. 150.

21. Discussion of the current debate over "artificial intelligence" is summarized by James Gleick in "Exploring the Labyrinth of the Mind," *The New York Times Magazine*, August 21, 1983, pp. 23–27, 83, 86–87, 100. General background exploring the question of artificial intelligence is provided by Douglas R. Hofstadter and Daniel C. Dennett, eds., *The Mind's I: Fantasies and Reflections on Self and Soul* (New York: Bantam Books, 1981). Also see Hofstadter's *Goedel, Escher, Bach: An Eternal Golden Braid* (New York: Basic Books, 1979).

22. Isaac Asimov, *I Robot* (New York: Doubleday, 1950). The scenario of humanity being taken over by superintelligent computers is explored at length by the Czech playwright and novelist Karel Čapek in his play, *R.U.R.* (Rossum's Universal Robots), written during the 1920s. In *R.U.R.* Čapek introduced the term "robot," which is synonymous in languages such as German with the idea of slave labor. Eventually in the play his robot characters take over the world. It should be noted that his robots were technically androids, having been evolved biologically rather than mechanically.

23. Asimov, *I Robot.*

24. David Bischoff, *WarGames,* based on the original screenplay by Lawrence Lasker and Walter F. Parkes (New York: Dell, 1983).

25. Clarke, *2010,* p. 201. The termination of HAL is also recounted in Clarke's *2001.*

26. Butler, *Erewhon,* p. 156.

Chapter 5. The Electronic Scriptorium

1. Elaine B. Kerr and Starr Roxanne Hiltz, *Computer-Mediated Communication Systems: Status and Evaluation* (New York: Academic Press, 1982), p. 3.
2. Detailed descriptions of a large number of these types of programs are outlined by Kerr and Hiltz.
3. Ibid., pp. 3–4.
4. Ibid., pp. 7–8.
5. Ibid., pp. 178–79.
6. Thomas S. Kuhn, *The Structure of Scientific Revolutions*, 2d ed. (Chicago: University of Chicago Press, 1970).
7. Daniel Bell, "The Information Society," in Michael L. Dertouzos and Joel Moses, eds., *The Computer Age: A Twenty-Year View* (Cambridge, Mass.: MIT Press, 1979), p. 190.
8. Quoted in Charles A. Thrall and Jerold M. Starr, eds., *Technology, Power and Social Change* (Carbondale and Edwardsville, Ill.: Southern Illinois University Press, 1972), p. 20.
9. Simon Nora and Alain Minc, *The Computerization of Society: A Report to the President of France* (Cambridge, Mass.: MIT Press, 1980), p. 79.
10. Ibid.
11. Marshall McLuhan, *Understanding Media: The Extensions of Man* (New York: Mentor Books, 1964), p. 85.

Chapter 6. Microcomputers and Colonialism

1. Daniel Bell, "The Information Society," In Michael L. Dertouzos and Joel Moses, eds., *The Computer Age: A Twenty-Year View* (Cambridge, Mass.: MIT Press, 1979), p. 168.
2. Edward A. Feigenbaum and Pamela McCorduck, *The Fifth Generation: Artificial Intelligence and Japan's Computer Challenge to the World* (Reading, Mass.: Addison-Wesley, 1983), p. 14.
3. Ibid.
4. Ibid., p. 2. Feigenbaum and McCorduck argue quite convincingly that Japan is involved in major competition with the United States to dominate the field of computer technology. Japan's reason for doing so seems to be based upon the conviction that computers and the knowledge systems they provide are the

key to economic power and control in the final decades of the twentieth century.

5. Ibid., p. 1.

6. Martin Carnoy, *Education as Cultural Imperialism* (New York: David McKay, 1974); Philip G. Altbach and Gail P. Kelly, *Education and Colonialism* (New York: Longman, 1978); Gail P. Kelly, "The Relation Between Colonial and Metropolitan Schools: A Structural Analysis," *Comparative Education* 15 (1979): 209–15.

7. Simon Nora and Alain Minc, *The Computerization of Society: A Report to the President of France* (Cambridge, Mass.: MIT Press, 1980).

8. Ibid., p. xv. Bell wrote the preface of the English edition.

9. Feigenbaum and McCorduck, *The Fifth Generation*, p. 14.

10. Nora and Minc, *The Computerization of Society*, p. 80.

11. Marshall McLuhan, *Understanding Media: The Extensions of Man* (New York: Mentor Books, 1964), p. 65.

12. Ibid., p. 83.

13. Nora and Minc, *The Computerization of Society*, p. 130.

14. Ibid., p. 6.

15. Ibid., p. 67.

16. McLuhan, *Understanding Media*, p. 75.

Chapter 7. Microcomputers and Education

1. Ernest Becker, *The Structure of Evil* (New York: Free Press, 1978), pp. 169–74.

2. Robert P. Taylor, "Introduction," in Robert P. Taylor, ed., *The Computer in the School: Tutor, Tool, Tutee* (New York: Teachers College Press, 1980), pp. 2–4.

3. Joseph Weizenbaum, "Another View from MIT," *BYTE: The Small Systems Journal* 9, no. 6 (June 1984): 225. Weizenbaum's views on computers and their impact on society are outlined in detail in his work, *Computer Power and Human Reason: From Judgment to Calculation* (San Francisco: W. H. Freeman, 1976).

4. Weizenbaum, "Another View from MIT," p. 225.

5. Ibid.

6. Seymour Papert, *Mindstorms: Children, Computers, and Powerful Ideas* (New York: Basic Books, 1980), p. 5. Emphasis in original.

7. Ibid. These ideas are outlined in detail in Papert's introduction, entitled "Computers for Children," pp. 3–18; and Chapter 1, "Computers and Computer Cultures," pp. 19–37.

8. Ibid., p. 9.

9. Ibid., p. 7.

10. Jean Piaget, *To Understand Is to Invent* and *The Future of Education* (New York: Penguin Books, 1972).

11. Papert, *Mindstorms*, p. 9. Emphasis in original.

12. Ibid., p. 21.

13. Jacques Ellul, *The Technological Society* (New York: Vintage Books, 1964), p. xxv. Emphasis in original.

14. Robert J. Sardello, "The Technological Threat to Education," in Douglas Sloan, ed., *The Computer in Education: A Critical Perspective* (New York: Teachers College Press, 1985), p. 95.

15. Ibid.

16. Douglas Sloan, "Introduction: On Raising Critical Questions About the Computer in Education," in Sloan, ed., *The Computer in Education*, p. 1.

17. Andrew Merton, "Computers in the Classroom," *Technology Illustrated* 3, no. 9 (September 1983): 46.

18. Sloan, "Raising Critical Questions," p. 3.

19. Simon Nora and Alain Minc, *The Computerization of Society: A Report to the President of France* (Cambridge, Mass.: MIT Press, 1980), p. 132.

20. Marshall McLuhan, *Understanding Media: The Extensions of Man* (New York: Mentor Books, 1964), pp. 75–76.

21. C. P. Snow, *The Two Cultures and the Scientific Revolution* (New York: Cambridge University Press, 1961), p. 4.

22. Ibid., p. 17.

23. Nora and Minc, *The Computerization of Society*, pp. 131–32.

24. The idea of the computer imposing a structure or language on the user is extremely interesting. Douglas Sloan of Teachers College, Columbia University, has suggested in our personal discussions that, for example, the fact that computers were originally developed for the military has determined to a certain extent the types of questions they have been able to address. Essentially, the matter reduces itself to whether or not knowledge and information are defined by the languages and systems we use to organize them.

25. Nora and Minc, *The Computerization of Society*, p. 139.

26. Ibid., p. 136.

27. Adam Schaff, "Occupation Versus Work," in Guenter

Friedrichs and Adam Schaff, eds., *Microelectronics and Society: A Report to the Club of Rome* (New York: New American Library, 1983), pp. 322–34.

28. Ibid., p. 332.

29. Ibid.

Chapter 8. Conclusion: Proteus and the Future of Intelligence

1. Marshall McLuhan, *The Gutenberg Galaxy: The Making of Typographic Man* (Toronto: University of Toronto Press, 1965), p. 12.

2. Marvin L. Minsky, "Computer Science and the Representation of Knowledge," in Michael L. Dertouzos and Joel Moses, eds., *The Computer Age: A Twenty-Year View* (Cambridge, Mass.: MIT Press, 1979), p. 397.

3. McLuhan, *The Gutenberg Galaxy*, pp. 278–79.

4. Simon Nora and Alain Minc, *The Computerization of Society: A Report to the President of France* (Cambridge, Mass.: MIT Press, 1980), p. 129.

5. Norbert Weiner's ideas are outlined in detail in his work *Cybernetics, or Control and Communication in the Animal and the Machine*, 2d ed. (Cambridge, Mass.: MIT Press, 1961). Originally published in 1948. Weiner later published a version of the work intended for a more general audience, entitled *The Human Use of Human Beings: Cybernetics and Society* (New York: Avon Books, 1967). Originally published in 1950.

6. Ibid., p. 24.

Bibliography

Altbach, Philip B. and Kelly, Gail P., *Education and Colonialism.* New York: Longman, 1978.

Asimov, Isaac. *I Robot.* New York: Doubleday, 1950.

Bischoff, David. *WarGames.* New York: Dell Books, 1983. Based on the original screenplay by Lawrence Lasker and Walter F. Parkes.

Becker, C. L. *Progress and Power.* Stanford, Calif.: Stanford University Press, 1936.

Becker, Ernest. *The Structure of Evil.* New York: Free Press, 1978.

Bell, Daniel. *The End of Ideology.* New York: Collier Books, 1961.

————. *The Coming of Post-Industrial Society: A Venture in Social Forecasting.* New York: Basic Books, 1973.

————, ed. *Towards the Year 2000: Work in Progress.* Boston: Beacon Press, 1968.

Bell, Daniel, and J. A. Mau, eds. *The Sociology of the Future.* New York: Harper & Row, 1972.

Bernstein, Jeremy. *The Analytical Engine: Computers—Past, Present and Future.* New York: Random House, 1978.

Boden, Margaret A. *Artificial Intelligence and Natural Man.* New York: Basic Books, 1977.

Bolter, J. David. *Turing's Man: Western Culture in the Computer Age.* Chapel Hill, N.C.: University of North Carolina Press, 1984.

Bowden, B. W. *Faster Than Thought: A Symposium on Digital Computer Machines.* London: Pitman, 1953.

Brad, Craig. *Techno Stress: The Human Cost of the Computer Revolution.* Reading, Mass.: Addison-Wesley, 1984.

Buckingham, Walter. *Automation: Its Impact on People and Business*. New York: New American Library, 1961.

Burnham, David. *The Rise of the Computer State*. New York: Random House, 1983.

Butler, Samuel. *Erewhon*. New York: Airmont, 1967.

Carnoy, Martin. *Education and Cultural Imperialism*. New York: David McKay, 1974.

Carter, John, and Percy H. Muir, eds. *Printing and the Mind of Man*. New York: Holt, Rinehart and Winston, 1967.

Clarke, Arthur C. *2001: A Space Odyssey*. New York: New American Library, 1968.

————. *Profiles of the Future: An Inquiry Into the Limits of the Possible*. New York: Popular Library, 1977.

————. *2010: Space Odyssey Two*. New York: Ballantine Books, 1982.

Cuffaro, Harriet. "Microcomputers in Education: Why Is Earlier Better?" In *The Computer in Education: A Critical Perspective*, edited by Douglas Sloan, pp. 21-30. New York: Teachers College Press, 1985.

Davy, John. "Mindstorms in the Lamplight." In *The Computer in Education: A Critical Perspective*, edited by Douglas Sloan, pp. 11-20. New York: Teachers College Press, 1985.

Dechaert, Charles E. *The Social Impact of Cybernetics*. New York: Simon and Schuster, 1966.

Deken, Joseph. *The Electronic Cottage*. New York: Bantam Books, 1981.

Dertouzos, Michael L., and Joel Moses, eds. *The Computer Age: A Twenty-Year View*. Cambridge, Mass.: MIT Press, 1979.

Dreyfus, Hubert L., and Stuart E. Dreyfus. "Putting Computers in Their Proper Place: Analysis Versus Intuition in the Classroom." In *The Computer in Education: A Critical Perspective*, edited by Douglas Sloan, pp. 40-63. New York: Teachers College Press, 1985.

Drucker, Peter F. *The Age of Discontinuity: Guidelines to Our Changing Society*. New York: Harper & Row, 1969.

Eames, Charles, and Ray Eames. *A Computer Perspective*, edited by Glen Fleck. Cambridge, Mass.: Harvard University Press, 1973.

Eisenstein, Elizabeth L. *The Printing Press as an Agent of Change: Communications and Cultural Transformations in Early-Modern Europe*, two volumes. Cambridge: Cambridge University Press, 1979.

Ellul, Jacques. *The Technological Society*. New York: Vintage Books, 1964.

Evans, Christopher. *The Micro Millennium*. New York: Viking Press, 1980.

―――. *The Making of the Micro: A History of the Computer*. New York: Van Nostrand Reinhold, 1981.

Febvre, Lucien, and Henri-Jean Martin. *The Coming of the Book: The Impact of Printing, 1450–1800*. Translated by David Gerard. London: NLB, 1976.

Fedeida, Am, and Rex Malik. *Viewdata Revolution*. New York: John Wiley, 1979.

Feigenbaum, Edward A., and Pamela McCorduck. *The Fifth Generation: Artificial Intelligence and Japan's Computer Challenge to the World*. Reading, Mass.: Addison-Wesley, 1983.

Foucault, Michel, *Power/Knowledge: Selected Interviews and Other Writings, 1972–1977*. Edited by Colin Gordon. New York: Pantheon Books, 1980.

Foucault, Michel. *Power/Knowledge: Selected Interviews and Other Writings, 1972–1977*. Edited by Colin Gordon. New York: Pantheon Books, 1980.

Friedrichs, Guenter, and Adam Schaff, eds. *Microelectronics and Society: A Report to the Club of Rome*. New York: New American Library, 1983.

Ganley, H. Oswald, and Gladys D. Ganley. *To Inform or Control? The New Communications Networks*. New York: McGraw-Hill, 1982.

Gleick, James. "Exploring the Labyrinth of the Mind." *The New York Times Magazine*, August 21, 1983, pp. 23–27, 83, 86–87, 100.

Gouldner, Alvin W. *The Future of Intellectuals and the Rise of the New Class*. New York: Seabury Press, 1979.

Greenfield, Patricia Marks. *Mind and Media: The Effects of Television, Video Games and Computers*. Cambridge, Mass.: Harvard University Press, 1984.

Hall, Edward T. *Beyond Culture*. New York: Anchor Books, 1977.

―――. *The Silent Language*. New York: Anchor Books, 1979.

Hofstadter, Douglas R. *Goedel, Escher, Bach: An Eternal Golden Braid*. New York: Basic Books, 1979.

Hofstadter, Douglas R., and Daniel C. Dennett, eds. *The Mind's I: Fantasies and Reflections on Self and Soul*. New York: Bantam Books, 1981.

Huxley, Aldous. *Brave New World*. New York: Harper & Row, 1969.

Innis, Harold A. *Empire and Communication*. Oxford: Oxford University Press, 1950.

————. *The Bias of Communication*. Toronto: University of Toronto Press, 1964.

Kelly, Gail P. "The Relation Between Colonial and Metropolitan Schools: A Structural Analysis." Comparative Education, 15 (1979): 209–15.

Kerr, Elaine B., and Starr Roxanne Hiltz. *Computer-Mediated Communication Systems: Status and Evaluation*. New York: Academic Press, 1982.

Kidder, Tracy. *The Soul of a New Machine*. New York: Avon Books, 1981.

Kuhn, Thomas S. *The Structure of Scientific Revolutions*. 2d ed. Chicago: University of Chicago Press, 1970.

Kumar, Krishan. *Prophecy and Progress: The Sociology of Industrial and Post-Industrial Society*. New York: Penguin Books, 1978.

Lumsden, Charles J., and Edward O. Wilson. *Promethean Fire: Reflections on the Origin of Mind*. Cambridge, Mass.: Harvard University Press, 1983.

Marchand, Donald A. *The Politics of Privacy, Computers, and Criminal Justice Records*. Arlington, Va.: Information Resources Press, 1980.

Martin, James. *The Wired Society: A Challenge for Tomorrow*. Englewood Cliffs, N.J.: Prentice-Hall, 1978.

Martin, James, and Adrian R. D. Norman. *The Computerized Society*. Englewood Cliffs, N.J.: Prentice-Hall, 1970.

McCorduck, Pamela. *Machines Who Think*. San Francisco: W. H. Freeman, 1979.

McGarry, K. J. *Communication, Knowledge and the Library*. London: Clive Bingley, 1975.

McLuhan, Marshall. *Understanding Media: The Extensions of Man*. New York: Mentor Books, 1964.

————. *The Gutenberg Galaxy: The Making of Typographic Man*. Toronto: University of Toronto Press, 1962.

————. *War and Peace in the Global Village*. New York: Bantam Books, 1968.

Menosky, Joseph. "Computer Literacy and the Press." In *The Computer in Education: A Critical Perspective*, edited by Douglas Sloan, pp. 77–83. New York: Teachers College Press, 1985.

Merton, Andrew. "Computers in the Classroom." *Technology Illustrated* 3, no. 9 (September 1983): 46.

Moore, Doris Langley. *Ada, Countess of Lovelace, Byron's Legitimate Daughter*. New York: Harper & Row, 1977.

Mowshowitz, Abbe. *The Conquest of Will: Information Processing in Human Affairs*. Reading, Mass.: Addison-Wesley, 1976.

Noble, Douglas. "Computer Literacy and Ideology." In *The Computer in Education: A Critical Perspective*, edited by Douglas Sloan, pp. 64–76. New York: Teachers College Press, 1985.

Nora, Simon, and Alain Minc. *The Computerization of Society: A Report to the President of France*. Cambridge, Mass.: MIT Press, 1980.

Orwell, George. *1984*. New York: Signet Library, 1961.

Papert, Seymour. *Mindstorms: Children, Computers and Power Ideas*. New York: Basic Books, 1980.

Pattison, Robert. *On Literacy: The Politics of the Word from Homer to the Age of Rock*. New York: Oxford University Press, 1982.

Piaget, Jean. *To Understand Is To Invent* and *The Future of Education*. New York: Penguin Books, 1972.

Pylyshyn, Zenon W., ed. *Perspectives on the Computer Revolution*. Englewood Cliffs, N.J.: Prentice-Hall, 1970.

Sardello, Robert J., "The Technological Threat to Education." In *The Computer in Education: A Critical Perspective*, edited by Douglas Sloan, pp. 93–101. New York: Teachers College Press, 1985.

Silverberg, Robert, ed. *The Science Fiction Hall of Fame*, vol. 1. New York: Avon Books, 1970.

Simpson, Brian. "Heading for the Ha-Ha." In *The Computer in Education: A Critical Perspective*, edited by Douglas Sloan, pp. 84–92. New York: Teachers College Press, 1985.

Skinner, B.F. *The Technology of Teaching*. New York: Appleton-Century-Crofts, 1968.

Sloan, Douglas. "On Raising Critical Questions About the Computer in Education." In *The Computer in Education: A Critical Perspective*, edited by Douglas Sloan, pp. 1–9. New York: Teachers College Press, 1985.

Snow, C. P. *The Two Cultures and the Scientific Revolution*. New York: Cambridge University Press, 1961.

Steiner, George. *In Bluebeard's Castle: Some Notes Towards the Redefinition of Culture*. New Haven, Conn.: Yale University Press, 1971.

Tavis, Irene, ed. *The Computer Impact.* Englewood Cliffs, N.J.: Prentice-Hall, 1970.

Taylor, Robert P., ed. *The Computer in the School: Tutor, Tool, Tutee.* New York: Teachers College Press, 1980.

Thomis, Malcom I. *The Luddites: Machine Breaking in Regency England.* Hamden, Conn.: Archon Books, 1970.

Thrall, Charles A., and Jerold M. Starr, eds. *Technology, Power, and Social Change.* Carbondale and Edwardsville, Ill.: Southern Illinois University Press, 1971.

Toffler, Alvin. *The Third Wave.* New York: Bantam Books, 1981.

Turkle, Sherry. *The Second Self: Computers and the Human Spirit.* New York: Simon and Schuster, 1984.

Weiner, Norbert. *Cybernetics, or Control and Communication in the Animal and the Machine,* 2d ed. Cambridge, Mass: MIT Press, 1961.

———. *God and Golem, Inc.: A Comment on Certain Points Where Cybernetics Impinges on Religion.* Cambridge, Mass.: MIT Press, 1964.

———. *The Human Use of Human Beings: Cybernetics and Society.* New York: Avon Books, 1967. Originally published in 1950.

Weizenbaum, Joseph. *Computer Power and Human Reason: From Judgment to Calculation.* San Francisco: W. H. Freeman, 1976.

———. "Another View from MIT." *BYTE: The Small Systems Journal* 9, no. 6 (June 1984): 225.

Westin, Alan F., and Michael A. Baker. *Databanks in a Free Society: Computers, Record-Keeping and Privacy.* New York: Quadrangle/New York Times Books, 1972.

Wicklein, John. *Electronic Nightmare: The New Communications and Freedom.* New York: Viking Press, 1979.

Williams, Raymond, ed. *Contact: Human Communication and Its History.* New York: Thames and Hudson, 1981.

Woolfe, Roger. *Videotex: The New Television/Telephone Information Services.* London: Heyden, 1980.

Zagonc, Arthur G. "Computer Pedagogy? Questions Concerning the New Educational Technology." In *The Computer in Education: A Critical Perspective,* edited by Douglas Sloan, pp. 31–39. New York: Teachers College Press, 1985.

Index